brilliant
Microsoft®
Excel 2003
POCKET BOOK

Joe Habraken

PEARSON
Prentice
Hall

Harlow, England • London • New York • Boston • San Francisco • Toronto
Sydney • Tokyo • Singapore • Hong Kong • Seoul • Taipei • New Delhi
Cape Town • Madrid • Mexico City • Amsterdam • Munich • Paris • Milan

I2109809

Pearson Education Limited
Edinburgh Gate
Harlow
Essex CM20 2JE
England

and Associated Companies throughout the world

Visit us on the World Wide Web at:
www.pearsoned.co.uk

Original edition appeared in, Microsoft® Office 2003 All-in-One, 1st edition, 0789729369 by Joe Habraken, published by Que Publishing, Copyright © Que Publishing.

ISBN-13: 978-0-13-175727-1
ISBN-10: 0-13-175727-X

British Library Cataloguing-in-Publication Data
A catalogue record for this book is available from the British Library

10 9 8 7 6 5 4 3 2 1
10 09 08 07 06

Typeset in 9.5pt Helvetica by 30
Printed and bound in Great Britain by Ashford Colour Press Ltd, Gosport, Hampshire

The Publisher's policy is to use paper manufactured from sustainable forests.

Brilliant Pocket Books

What you need to know – when you need it!

When you're working on your PC and come up against a problem that you're unsure how to solve, or want to accomplish something in an application that you aren't sure how to do, where do you look? If you are fed up with wading through pages of background information in unwieldy manuals and training guides trying to find the piece of information or advice that you need RIGHT NOW, and if you find that helplines really aren't that helpful, then Brilliant Pocket Books are the answer!

Brilliant Pocket Books have been developed to allow you to find the info that you need easily and without fuss and to guide you through each task using a highly visual step-by-step approach – providing exactly what you need to know, when you need it!

Brilliant Pocket Books are concise, easy-to-access guides to all of the most common important and useful tasks in all of the applications in the Office 2003 suite. Short, concise lessons make it really easy to learn any particular feature, or master any task or problem that you will come across in day-to-day use of the applications.

When you are faced with any task on your PC, whether major or minor, that you are unsure about, your Brilliant Pocket Book will provide you with the answer – almost before you know what the question is!

Contents

Introduction   ix

1 Creating a New Workbook   1
→ Starting Excel   1
→ Understanding the Excel Window   1
→ Starting a New Workbook   4
→ Saving and Naming a Workbook   6
→ Saving a Workbook Under a New Name or Location   8
→ Opening an Existing Workbook   8
→ Closing Workbooks   9
→ Exiting Excel   10

2 Entering Data into the Worksheet   11
→ Understanding Excel Data Types   11
→ Entering Text   12
 – Tips on Entering Column and Row Labels   13
 – Adding Comments to Cells   14
→ Entering Numbers   16
→ Entering Dates and Times   17
→ Copying Data to Other Cells   18
 – Entering a Series of Numbers, Dates, and Other Data   19
 – Entering a Custom Series   20
→ Taking Advantage of AutoComplete   21

3 Performing Simple Calculations   23
→ Understanding Excel Formulas   23
 – Formula Operators   24
 – Order of Operations   25
→ Entering Formulas   25
→ Using the Status Bar AutoCalculate Feature   27
→ Displaying Formulas   28
→ Editing Formulas   29

4 Manipulating Formulas and Understanding Cell References   **31**

→ Copying Formulas   31
→ Using Relative and Absolute Cell Addresses   33
→ Recalculating the Worksheet   36

5 Performing Calculations with Functions   **37**

→ What Are Functions?   37
   – Using AutoSum   39
→ Using the Insert Function Feature   40

6 Getting Around in Excel   **45**

→ Moving from Worksheet to Worksheet   45
→ Switching Between Workbooks   46
→ Moving Within a Worksheet   47
   – Using the Keyboard   47
   – Using a Mouse   48
   – Using a Wheel-Enabled Mouse   49

7 Different Ways to View Your Worksheet   **51**

→ Changing the Worksheet View   51
→ Freezing Column and Row Labels   52
→ Splitting Worksheets   54
→ Hiding Workbooks, Worksheets, Columns, and Rows   55
→ Locking Cells in a Worksheet   56

8 Editing Worksheets   **59**

→ Correcting Data   59
→ Undoing an Action   60
→ Using the Replace Feature   60
→ Checking Your Spelling   63
→ Copying and Moving Data   64
   – Using Drag and Drop   65
   – Moving Data   66
   – Using Drag and Drop to Move Data   66
→ Using the Office Clipboard   66
→ Deleting Data   68

9   Changing How Numbers and Text Look   69

→ Formatting Text and Numbers   69
→ Using the Style Buttons to Format Numbers   69
→ Numeric Formatting Options   70
→ How You Can Make Text Look Different   73
→ Changing Text Attributes with Toolbar Buttons   74
→ Accessing Different Font Attributes   75
→ Aligning Text in Cells   76
    – Aligning Text from the Toolbar   77
    – Combining Cells and Wrapping Text   78
→ Copying Formats with Format Painter   79

10 Adding Cell Borders and Shading   81

→ Adding Borders to Cells   81
→ Adding Shading to Cells   83
→ Using AutoFormat   84
→ Applying Conditional Formatting   85

11 Working with Ranges   89

→ What Is a Range?   89
→ Selecting a Range   89
→ Naming Ranges   91
→ Creating Range Names from Worksheet Labels   93
→ Inserting a Range Name into a Formula or Function   93

12 Inserting and Removing Cells, Rows, and Columns   95

→ Inserting Rows and Columns   95
→ Removing Rows and Columns   96
→ Inserting Cells   97
→ Removing Cells   98
→ Adjusting Column Width and Row Height with a Mouse   99
→ Using the Format Menu for Precise Control   100

13 Managing Your Worksheets   103

→ Selecting Worksheets   103
→ Inserting Worksheets   104
→ Deleting Worksheets   106
→ Moving and Copying Worksheets   106

– Moving a Worksheet Within a Workbook with Drag
and Drop   107
– Moving or Copying a Worksheet Between Workbooks
with Drag and Drop   107
→ Changing Worksheet Tab Names   109

14 Printing Your Workbook   111

→ Previewing a Print Job   111
→ Changing the Page Setup   112
– Printing Column and Row Labels on Every Page   113
– Scaling a Worksheet to Fit on a Page   114
– Adding Headers and Footers   115
– Setting Sheet Settings   117
→ Printing Your Workbook   118
→ Selecting a Large Worksheet Print Area   120
→ Adjusting Page Breaks   120

15 Creating Charts   123

→ Understanding Charting Terminology   123
→ Working with Different Chart Types   124
→ Creating and Saving a Chart   125
→ Moving and Resizing a Chart   127
→ Printing a Chart   128

Introduction

Welcome to the *Brilliant Microsoft® Excel Pocket Book* – a handy visual quick reference that will give you a basic grounding in the common features and tasks that you will need to master to use Microsoft® Excel 2003 in any day-to-day situation. Keep it on your desk, in your briefcase or bag – or even in your pocket! – and you will always have the answer to hand for any problem or task that you come across.

Find out what you need to know – when you need it!

You don't have to read this book in any particular order. It is designed so that you can jump in, get the information you need and jump out – just look up the task in the contents list, turn to the right page, read the introduction, follow the step-by-step instructions – and you're done!

How this book works

Each section in this book includes foolproof step-by-step instructions for performing specific tasks, using screenshots to illustrate each step. Additional information is included to help increase your understanding and develop your skills – these are identified by the following icons:

 Jargon buster – New or unfamiliar terms are defined and explained in plain English to help you as you work through a section.

 Timesaver tip – These tips give you ideas that cut corners and confusion. They also give you additional information related to the topic that you are currently learning. Use them to expand your knowledge of a particular feature or concept.

 Important – This identifies areas where new users often run into trouble, and offers practical hints and solutions to these problems.

Brilliant Pocket Books **are a handy, accessible resource that you will find yourself turning to time and time again when you are faced with a problem or an unfamiliar task and need an answer at your fingertips – or in your pocket!**

1 Creating a New Workbook

In this lesson, you learn how to start and exit Excel and you become familiar with the Excel window. You also learn how to create new workbooks and open existing workbook files.

→ Starting Excel

Excel is a spreadsheet program that can help you create worksheets and invoices and do simple and sophisticated number crunching; it is designed to help you calculate the results of formulas and help you organize and analyze numerical data.

To start Excel from the Windows desktop, follow these steps:

1 Click the **Start** button, and the Start menu appears.

2 Point at **All Programs** (in Windows XP; in Windows 2000 select **Programs**), and the Programs menu appears.

3 Select the **Microsoft Office** program group and then **Microsoft Office Excel 2003** to start the program.

→ Understanding the Excel Window

When you click the Microsoft Excel icon, the Excel application window appears, displaying a blank workbook labeled Book1 (see Figure 1.1). On the right side of the Excel window is the Getting Started task pane. This task pane enables you to connect to Microsoft online. It also allows you to open existing Excel workbooks or create new workbooks (which is discussed later in the lesson).

When you work in Excel, you use workbook files to hold your numerical data, formulas, and other objects, such as Excel charts. Each Excel workbook can consist of several sheets; each sheet is called a worksheet.

You enter your numbers and formulas on one of the workbook's worksheets. Each worksheet consists of 256 columns. The columns begin with column A and proceed through the alphabet. The 27th column is AA, followed by AB, AC, and this convention for naming subsequent columns continues through the entire alphabet until you end up with the last column (column 256), which is designated IV.

Each worksheet also consists of 65,536 rows. The intersection of a column and a row on the worksheet is called a cell. Each cell has an address that consists of the column and row that intersect to make the cell. For example, the very first cell on a worksheet is in column A and row 1, so the cell's address is A1.

Jargon buster

Cell Where a row and column intersect, each cell has an address that consists of the column letter and row number (A1, B3, C4, and so on). You enter data and formulas in the cells to create your worksheets.

Figure 1.1 shows cell A1 highlighted in worksheet 1 (designated as Sheet1 on its tab) of Workbook 1 (designated in the title bar as Book1; this will change to a particular filename after you name the workbook using the Save function).

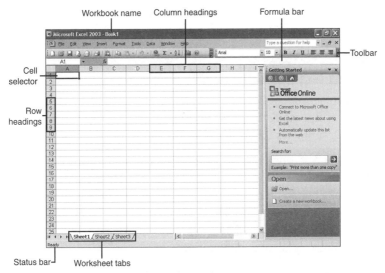

Figure 1.1 Excel provides a new workbook and the menus and toolbars necessary for doing some serious number crunching.

The Excel window shown here includes many of the various elements available in other Office applications, such as Word or PowerPoint. These elements include a menu bar (from which you select commands), a status bar (which displays the status of the current activity), and toolbars (which contain buttons and drop-down lists that provide quick access to various commands and features).

In addition, the window contains several elements that are unique to Excel, as shown in Table 1.1.

Table 1.1 Elements of the Excel Window

Element	Description
Formula bar	When you enter information into a cell, it appears in the Formula bar. You can use the Formula bar to edit the data later. The cell's location also appears in the Formula bar.
Column headings	The letters across the top of the worksheet, which identify the columns in the worksheet.
Row headings	The numbers down the side of the worksheet, which identify the rows in the worksheet.
Cell selector	The dark outline that indicates the active cell. (It highlights the cell you are currently working in.)
Worksheet tabs	These tabs help you move from worksheet to worksheet within the workbook.

→ Starting a New Workbook

As you've already seen, when you start Excel, it opens a new blank workbook. It is ready to accept data entry, which is discussed in Lesson 2, "Entering Data into the Worksheet."

The empty workbook that appears when you start Excel is pretty much a blank canvas, but Excel also enables you to create new workbooks based on a template. A *template* is a predesigned workbook that you can modify to suit your needs. Excel contains templates for creating invoices, expense reports, and other common business accounting forms.

To create a new workbook, follow these steps:

1 Open the **File** menu and select **New**. The New Workbook task pane appears on the right side of the Excel window (if you did not close it as outlined earlier, it should already be open).

2 The New Workbook task pane enables you to create new blank workbooks or create workbooks based on an existing workbook or a template (see Figure 1.2).

1

Figure 1.2 The New Workbook task pane provides quick access to commands for creating new Excel workbooks.

3 To create a blank workbook, click the **Blank Workbook** icon. A new blank workbook opens in the Excel window.

Timesaver tip

Instant Workbook You can also quickly start a new blank workbook by clicking the **New** button on the Standard toolbar.

Blank templates are fine when you have a design in mind for the overall look of the workbook. However, for some help with workbook layout and formatting, you can base your new workbook on an Excel template. To use an Excel template, follow these steps:

1 Click the **On My Computer** link in the Templates pane of the New Workbook task pane. The Templates dialog box appears.

2 Click the **Spreadsheet Solutions** tab on the Templates dialog box. The various workbook template icons appear (see Figure 1.3).

Figure 1.3 The Spreadsheet Solutions templates.

3 Select a template by clicking its icon, and then click **OK** or press **Enter**. A new workbook opens onscreen with a default name based on the template you chose. For example, if you chose the Timecard template, the new workbook is named Timecard1, as shown at the top of Figure 1.4.

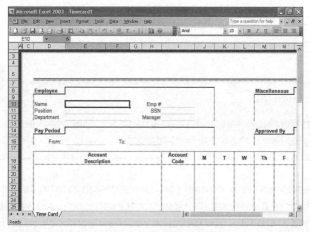

Figure 1.4 A new workbook based on a template provides a basic layout for a particular business form.

→ Saving and Naming a Workbook

Whether you build your workbook from a blank template or use one of the Excel templates, after you enter some data into the workbook, you should save the file (you learn about data entry in Lesson 2). Also, because changes that you make to the workbook are not automatically saved, you should occasionally save the edited version of your work.

The first time you save a workbook, you must name it and specify a location where it should be saved. Follow these steps to save your workbook:

1 Open the **File** menu and select **Save**, or click the **Save** button on the Standard toolbar. The Save As dialog box appears (see Figure 1.5).

2 Type the name you want to give the workbook in the **File Name** text box. You can use up to 218 characters, including any combination of letters, numbers, and spaces.

3 Normally, Excel saves your workbooks in the My Documents folder. To save the file to a different folder or drive (such as a network drive), select a new location using the **Save In** list.

Figure 1.5 Specify the name and location for your new workbook in the Save As dialog box.

Important

The Folder I Want to Save In Doesn't Exist! You can create a new folder from the Save As dialog box: click the **Create New Folder** button on the toolbar of the Save As dialog box, type a name for the new folder, and then press **Enter**.

4 Click **Save** to save your workbook and close the Save As dialog box.

To save changes that you make to a workbook that you have previously saved, just click the **Save** button on the Standard toolbar. You can also press the shortcut key combination of **Ctrl+S** to save changes to your workbook.

→ Saving a Workbook Under a New Name or Location

There might be an occasion when you want to save a copy of a particular workbook under a different name or in a different location. Excel makes it easy for you to make duplicates of a workbook. Follow these steps:

1 Select the **File** menu and select **Save As**. The Save As dialog box opens, just as if you were saving the workbook for the first time.

2 To save the workbook under a new name, type the new filename over the existing name in the **File Name** text box.

3 To save the new file on a different drive or in a different folder, select the drive letter or the folder from the **Save In** list.

4 To save the new file in a different format (such as WK4, which is a Lotus 1-2-3 format), click the **Save As Type** drop-down arrow and select the desired format.

5 Click the **Save** button or press **Enter**.

Timesaver tip

Saving Excel Workbooks in Other File Formats Occasionally, you might share Excel workbook data with coworkers or colleagues who don't use Excel. Being able to save Excel workbooks in other file formats, such as Lotus 1-2-3 (as discussed in step 4), enables you to provide another user a file that they can open in their spreadsheet program.

→ Opening an Existing Workbook

If you have a workbook you've previously saved that you would like to work on, you must open the file first, before you can make any changes. Follow these steps to open an existing workbook:

 1 Open the **File** menu and select **Open**, or click the **Open** button on the Standard toolbar. The Open dialog box shown in Figure 1.6 appears.

Figure 1.6 Use the Open dialog box to locate and open an existing Excel workbook.

2 If the file is not located in the current folder, open the **Look In** drop-down list box and select the correct drive and folder.

3 Select the file you want to open in the files and folders list.

4 To see a preview of the workbook before you open it, click the **Views** button and select **Preview**. Excel displays the contents of the workbook in a window to the right of the dialog box.

5 Click **Open** to open the currently selected workbook.

Timesaver tip

Recently Used Workbooks If the workbook you want to open is one of your four most recently used workbooks, you'll find it listed at the bottom of the File menu. It will also be listed at the top of the New Workbook task pane (if the task pane is active).

→ Closing Workbooks

When you have finished with a particular workbook and want to continue working in Excel, you can easily close the current workbook. Click the **Close** (**X**) button in the upper-right corner of the workbook. (There are two Close buttons; the one on top closes Excel, and the one below it closes the current workbook window.) You can also close the current workbook by selecting **File**, **Close**. If you have changed the workbook since the last time you saved it, you will be prompted to save any changes.

Timesaver tip

It's Closing Time! If you have more than one workbook open, you can close all of them at once by holding down the **Shift** key, selecting the **File** menu, and then selecting **Close All**.

→ Exiting Excel

When you have finished working with Excel, you need to exit the application. This closes all workbooks that are currently open. To exit Excel, select the **File** menu and select **Exit**. Or you can click the **Close** (**X**) button at the upper-right corner of the Excel window.

If you have changed any of the workbooks that you were working with, you are prompted to save changes to these workbook files before exiting Excel.

2 Entering Data into the Worksheet

In this lesson, you learn how to enter different types of data into an Excel worksheet.

→ Understanding Excel Data Types

When you work in Excel, you enter different types of information, such as text, numbers, dates, times, formulas, and functions (which is a special built-in formula provided by Excel). Excel data basically comes in two varieties: labels and values.

A label is a text entry; it is called a label because it typically provides descriptive information such as the name of a person, place, or thing. A label has no numerical significance in Excel; it's just there to describe accompanying values.

Jargon buster

Label Any text entry made on an Excel worksheet.

A value is data that has numerical significance. This includes numbers, dates, and times that you enter on your worksheet. Values can be acted on by formulas and functions. Formulas are discussed in Lesson 3, "Performing Simple Calculations," and Excel functions in Lesson 5, "Performing Calculations with Functions."

Jargon buster

Values Entries, such as numbers and dates, that have numerical significance and can be acted upon by formulas or functions.

→ Entering Text

Text is any combination of letters, numbers, and spaces. By default, text is automatically left-aligned in a cell, whereas numerical data is right-aligned.

Timesaver tip

Entering Numbers As Text To enter a number that you want treated as text (such as a ZIP code), precede the entry with a single quotation mark ('), as in '46220. The single quotation mark is an alignment prefix that tells Excel to treat the following characters as text and left-align them in the cell. You do not have to do this to "text" numerical entries, but it ensures that they will not be mistakenly acted upon by formulas or functions.

To enter text into a cell, follow these steps:

1 Use your mouse or the keyboard arrows to select the cell in which you want to enter text.

2 Type the text. As you type, your text appears in the cell and in the Formula bar, as shown in Figure 2.1.

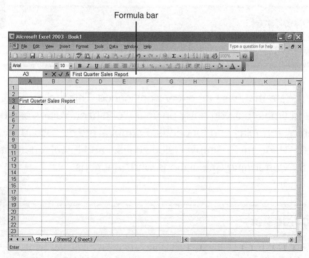

Figure 2.1 Data that you enter into a cell also appears in the Formula bar as you type it.

3 Press **Enter**. Your text appears in the cell, left-aligned. The cell selector moves down one cell. You can also press **Tab** or an arrow key to enter the text and move to the next cell to the right (or in the direction of the arrow).

2

> ## Important
>
> **!**
>
> **But My Entry Doesn't Fit!** When text does not fit into a cell (because of the column width set for that column), Excel displays the information in one of two ways: If the next cell is empty, the text overflows into that cell, allowing you to see your entire entry. If the cell to the right of your entry is not empty, you will be able to see only the portion of your entry that fits within the confines of the cell. This can easily be remedied by changing the column width. You learn about changing column widths in Lesson 12, "Inserting and Removing Cells, Rows, and Columns."

Tips on Entering Column and Row Labels

Column and row labels identify your data. Column labels appear across the top of the worksheet beneath the worksheet title (if any). Row labels are entered on the left side of the worksheet.

Column labels describe what the numbers in a column represent. Typically, column labels specify time intervals such as years, months, days, quarters, and so on. Row labels describe what the numbers in each row represent. Typically, row labels specify data categories, such as product names, employee names, or income and expense items in a budget.

When entering your column labels, enter the first label and press the **Tab** key instead of pressing Enter. This moves you to the next cell on the right so that you can enter another column label. When entering row labels, use the down-arrow key or Enter instead of the Tab key. Figure 2.2 shows the various labels for a quarterly sales summary.

Column labels

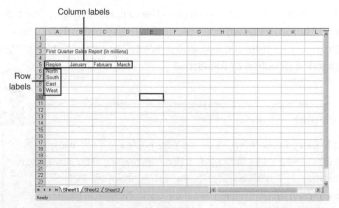

Figure 2.2 Column and row headings serve as labels for the data you enter on the worksheet.

If you need to enter similar data (such as a series of months or years) as column or row labels, you can enter them quickly as a series; this technique is discussed later in this lesson.

Adding Comments to Cells

You can add comments to particular cells, although the comments are not really considered cell content (such as labels and values). These comments allow you to associate information with a cell—information that does not appear (by default) with the worksheet when sent to the printer.

Comments are similar to placing a Post-it note on a cell, reminding you that an outstanding issue is related to that cell. For example, if you need to check the value that you've placed in a particular cell to make sure that it's accurate, you can place a comment in the cell (see Figure 2.3). Cells containing comments are marked with a red triangle in the upper-right corner of the cell. To view a comment, place the mouse pointer on the comment triangle.

Red triangle indicates a
comment in that cell

Comment box

Figure 2.3 Comments can be added to cells as a kind of electronic Post-it note.

To insert a comment into a cell, follow these steps:

1 Click the cell in which you want to place the comment.

2 Select **Insert, Comment**. A comment box appears next to the cell.

3 Type your information into the comment box.

4 Click anywhere else in the worksheet to close the comment box.

You can also easily remove comments from cells. Select the cell, and then select **Edit** and point at **Clear**. On the cascading menu, select **Comments** to remove the comment.

Timesaver tip

Right-Click a Cell to Add Comment You can add a comment to a cell by right-clicking on the cell and then selecting **Insert Comment** from the shortcut menu that appears.

→ Entering Numbers

Data that serves as the values in your workbooks can include the numeric characters 0–9. Because formulas are also considered values (you learn about simple calculations in Lesson 3), other valid value characters include symbols such as +, –, /, and *. You can also use characters such as a comma (,), a percent sign (%), or a dollar sign ($) in your values. You will find, however, that you can save yourself a few data-entry keystrokes and add these characters using different Excel formatting options (you learn about Excel formatting in Lesson 9, "Changing How Numbers and Text Look").

For example, you could enter the dollar amount $700.00 including the dollar sign and the decimal point. However, it's probably faster to enter the 700 into the cell and then format all the cells that contain dollar amounts after you have entered all the data.

To enter a value, follow these steps:

1 Click in the cell where you want to enter the value.

2 Type the value. To enter a negative number, precede it with a minus sign or surround it with parentheses.

3 Press **Enter** or the **Tab** key; the value appears in the cell right-aligned. Figure 2.4 shows various values entered into a simple worksheet.

Timesaver tip

What Are All Those Pound Signs? If you enter a number and it appears in the cell as all pound signs (#######) or in scientific notation (such as 7.78E+06), the cell just isn't wide enough to display the entire number. To fix it, double-click the right border of the column's heading. The column expands to fit the largest entry in that column. See Lesson 12 for more information on working with column widths.

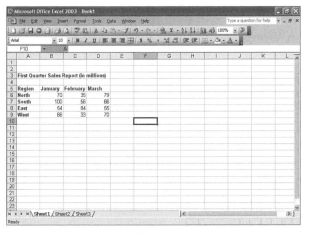

Figure 2.4 Values are right-aligned in a cell.

→ Entering Dates and Times

Dates that you enter into an Excel workbook have numerical significance. Excel converts the date into a number that reflects the number of days that have elapsed since January 1, 1900. Even though you won't see this number (Excel displays your entry as a normal date), the number is used whenever you use this date in a calculation. Times are also considered values. Excel sees them as the number of seconds that have passed since 12 a.m.

Follow these steps to enter a date or time:

1 Click in the cell where you want to enter a date or a time.

2 To enter a date, use the format MM/DD/YY or the format MM-DD-YY, as in 5/9/03 or 5-9-03.

To enter a time, be sure to specify a.m. or p.m., as in 7:21 p or 8:22 a.

Timesaver tip

A.M. or P.M.? Unless you type am or pm after your time entry, Excel assumes that you are using a 24-hour international clock. Therefore, 8:20 is assumed to be a.m., not p.m. (20:20 would be p.m.: 8 plus 12 hours). Therefore, if you mean p.m., type the entry as 8:20 pm (or 8:20 p). Note that you must type a space between the time and the am or pm notation.

3 Press **Enter**. As long as Excel recognizes the entry as a date or a time, it appears right-aligned in the cell. If Excel doesn't recognize it, it's treated as text and left-aligned.

After you enter your date or time, you can format the cells to display the date or time exactly as you want it to appear, such as September 16, 2003, or 16:50 (international time). If you're entering a column of dates or times, you can format the entire column in one easy step. To format a column, click the column header to select the column. Then open the **Format** menu and select **Cells**. On the **Numbers** tab, select the date or time format you want to use (you learn more about formatting text and numbers in Lesson 9).

→ Copying Data to Other Cells

Another way to enter labels or values onto a sheet is to use the Fill feature. You can copy (fill) an entry into surrounding cells. For example, suppose you have a list of salespeople on a worksheet, and they will each get a $100 bonus. You can enter the 100 once and then use the Fill feature to insert multiple copies of 100 into nearby cells. To use the Fill feature for copying, follow these steps:

1 Click the fill handle of the cell (the small block in the lower-right corner of the cell) that holds the data that you want to copy (see Figure 2.5).

2 Drag the fill handle down or to the right to copy the data to adjacent cells. A data tag appears to let you know exactly what data is being copied into the cells.

3 Release the mouse button. The data is "filled" into the selected cells.

When you release the mouse, a shortcut box for Fill options appears at the end of the cells that you filled. Copy Cells is the default option for the Fill feature, so you can ignore the shortcut box for the moment. It does come into play when you enter a series in the next section.

Information

Watch That Fill! The data you're copying replaces any existing data in the adjacent cells that you fill.

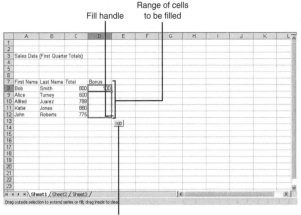

Figure 2.5 Drag the fill handle to copy the contents of a cell into neighboring cells.

Entering a Series of Numbers, Dates, and Other Data

Entering a value *series* (such as January, February, and March or 1, 2, 3, 4, and so on) is accomplished using the Fill feature discussed in the preceding section. When you use the Fill feature, Excel looks at the cell holding the data and tries to determine whether you want to just copy that information into the adjacent cells or use it as the starting point for a particular series of data. For example, with Monday entered in the first cell of the series, Excel automatically inserts Tuesday, Wednesday, and so on into the adjacent cells when you use the Fill feature.

Sometimes Excel isn't quite sure whether you want to copy the data when you use Fill or create a series. This is where the Fill options shortcut box comes in. It enables you to select how the Fill feature should treat the data that you have "filled" into the adjacent cells. Figure 2.6 shows the creation of a data series using Fill.

When you create a series using Fill, the series progresses by one increment. For example, a series starting with 1 would proceed to 2, 3, 4, and so on. If you want to create a series that uses some increment other than 1, you must create a custom series.

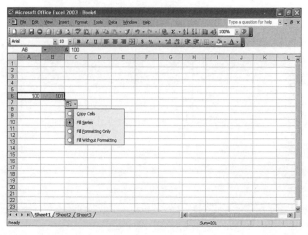

Figure 2.6 Fill can also be used to create a series of data in adjacent cells.

Entering a Custom Series

If you want to create a series such as 10, 20, 30, where the series uses
a custom increment between the values, you need to create a custom
series. Excel provides two ways to create a custom series. To create a
custom series using Fill, follow these steps:

1 Enter the first value in the series into a cell.

2 Enter the second value in the series into the next cell. For
example, you might enter **10** into the first cell and then **20** into the
second cell. This lets Excel know that the increment for the series
is 10.

3 Select both cells by clicking the first cell and dragging over the
second cell.

4 Drag the fill handle of the second cell to the other cells that will
be part of the series. Excel analyzes the two cells, sees the
incremental pattern, and re-creates it in subsequent cells.

You can also create a custom series using the Series dialog box. This
enables you to specify the increment or step value for the series and
even specify a stop value for the series.

1 Enter the first value in the series into a cell.

2 Select the cells that you want included in the series.

3 Select the **Edit** menu, point at **Fill**, and then select **Series**. The
Series dialog box opens (see Figure 2.7).

Figure 2.7 The Series dialog box enables you to create a custom series.

4 Enter the Step Value for the series. You can also enter a Stop Value for the series if you did not select the cells used for the series in step 2. For example, if you want to add a series to a column of cells and have clicked in the first cell that will receive a value, using a Stop Value (such as 100 for a series that will go from 1 to 100) will "stop" entering values in the cells when it reaches 100—the Stop Value.

5 Click **OK** to create the series.

Timesaver tip

Different Series Types Not only can you create a linear series using the Series dialog box (as discussed in the steps in this section), but you can also create growth and date series. In a growth series, the data you're copying replaces any existing data in the adjacent cells that you fill.

→ Taking Advantage of AutoComplete

Another useful feature that Excel provides to help take some of the drudgery out of entering information into a workbook is the AutoComplete feature. Excel keeps a list of all the labels that you enter on a worksheet by column. For example, suppose you have a worksheet tracking sales in Europe and you are entering country names, such as Germany, Italy, and so on, multiple times into a particular column in the worksheet. After you enter Germany the first time, it becomes part of the AutoComplete list for that column. The next time you enter the letter G into a cell in that column, Excel completes the entry as "Germany."

You can also select an entry from the AutoComplete list. This allows you to see the entire list of available entries. Follow these steps:

1 Enter your text and value data as needed onto the worksheet.

2 If you want to select a text entry from the AutoComplete list, to fill an empty cell, right-click that cell. A shortcut menu appears.

3 Select **Pick from List** from the shortcut menu. A list of text entries (in alphabetical order) appears below the current cell.

4 Click a word in the list to insert it into the current, empty cell.

Timesaver tip

Adding Data to Excel Using Voice Recognition The Office Speech Recognition feature can also be used to enter data into an Excel worksheet and to perform voice commands. If you have a computer that is set up with a sound card and microphone, you can use this feature.

3 Performing Simple Calculations

In this lesson, you learn how to use formulas to calculate results in your worksheets.

→ Understanding Excel Formulas

One way to add calculations to an Excel workbook is to create your own formulas. Formulas are typically used to perform calculations such as addition, subtraction, multiplication, and division. More complex calculations are better left to Excel functions, which is a built-in set of formulas that provide financial, mathematical, and statistical calculations. You learn more about functions in Lesson 5, "Performing Calculations with Functions."

Formulas that you create typically include cell addresses that reference cells on which you want to perform a calculation. Formulas also consist of mathematical operators, such as + (addition) or * (multiplication). For example, if you wanted to multiply two cells, such as C3 and D3, and then divide the product by 3, you would design a formula that looks like this:

=(C3*D3)/3

Notice that the formula begins with the equal sign (=). This lets Excel know that the information that you are placing in the cell is meant to do a calculation. The parentheses are used to let Excel know that you want C3 multiplied by D3 before the result is divided by 3. Creating appropriate formulas requires an understanding of the order of mathematical operations, or what is often called the rules of precedence. The natural order of math operations is covered in the next section.

Formula Operators

As previously mentioned, you can create formulas that add, subtract, and multiply cells in the worksheet. Table 3.1 lists some of the operators that you can use and how you would use them in a simple formula.

Table 3.1   Excel's Mathematical Operators

Operator	Performs	Sample Formula	Result
^	Exponentiation	=A1^3	Enters the result of raising the value in cell A1 to the third power
+	Addition	=A1+A2	Enters the total of the values in cells A1 and A2
–	Subtraction	=A1–A2	Subtracts the value in cell A2 from the value in cell A1
*	Multiplication	=A2*A3	Multiplies the value in cell A2 by cell A3
/	Division	=A1/B1	Divides the value in cell A1 by the value in cell B1

Figure 3.1 shows some formulas that have been created for an Excel worksheet. So that you can see how I wrote the formulas, I've configured Excel so that it shows the formula that has been placed in a cell rather than the results of the formula (which is what you would normally see).

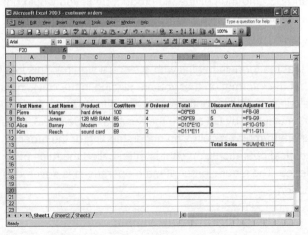

Figure 3.1 You can create formulas to do simple calculations in your worksheets.

Order of Operations

The order of operations, or *operator precedence*, simply means that some operations take precedence over other operations in a formula. For example, in the formula =C2+D2*E2, the multiplication of D2 times E2 takes precedence, so D2 is multiplied by E2 and then the value in cell C2 is added to the result.

You can force the precedence of an operation by using parentheses. For example, if you want C2 and D2 added before they are multiplied by E2, the formula would have to be written =(C2+D2)*E2.

The natural order of math operators follows:

1 Exponent (^) and calculations within parentheses

2 Multiplication (*) and division (/)

3 Addition (+) and subtraction (−)

In the case of operations such as multiplication and division, which operate at the same level in the natural order, a formula containing the multiplication operator followed by the division operator will execute these operators in the order they appear in the formula from left to right. If you don't take this order into consideration, you could run into problems when entering your formulas. For example, if you want to determine the average of the values in cells A1, B1, and C1, and you enter **=A1+B1+C1/3**, you'll get the wrong answer. The value in C1 will be divided by 3, and that result will be added to A1+B1. To determine the total of A1 through C1 first, you must enclose that group of values in parentheses: **=(A1+B1+C1)/3**.

→ Entering Formulas

You can enter formulas in one of two ways: by typing the entire formula, including the cell addresses, or by typing the formula operators and selecting the cell references. Take a look at both ways.

To type a formula, perform the following steps:

1 Select the cell where you will place the formula.

2 Type an equal sign (=) into the cell to begin the formula.

3 Enter the appropriate cell references and operators for the formula. Figure 3.2 shows a simple multiplication formula. The formula also appears in the Formula bar as you type it. The cells that you specify in the formula are highlighted with a colored border.

4 Press **Enter** when you have finished the formula, and Excel calculates the result.

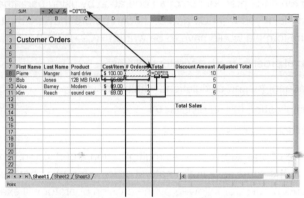

Cell border and cell text reference have matching color

Figure 3.2 The formula appears in the cell and in the Formula bar as you type it.

Timesaver tip

Unwanted Formula If you start to enter a formula and then decide you don't want to use it, you can skip entering the formula by pressing **Esc**.

To enter a formula by selecting cell addresses, follow these steps:

1 Click in the cell where you will place the formula.

2 Type the equal sign (=) to begin the formula.

3 Click the cell whose address you want to appear first in the formula. You can also click a cell in a different worksheet or workbook. The cell address appears in the cell and in the Formula bar.

4 Type a mathematical operator after the value to indicate the next operation you want to perform. The operator appears in the cell and in the Formula bar.

5 Continue clicking cells and typing operators until the formula is complete.

6 Press **Enter** to accept the formula and have Excel place its results into the cell.

Important

Error! If ERR appears in a cell, you probably made a mistake somewhere in the formula. Be sure you did not commit one of these common errors: dividing by zero, using a blank cell as a divisor, referring to a blank cell, deleting a cell used in a formula, or including a reference to the same cell in which the formula appears.

Timesaver tip

Natural Language Formulas Excel also enables you to create what are called Natural Language formulas. You can refer to a cell by its column heading name and the corresponding row label. For example, if you had a column labeled Total and a column labeled Discount for each customer, you can write a formula such as =Smith Total–Smith Discount. You are referring to cells by the labels that you have placed in the worksheet rather than the actual cell addresses.

→ Using the Status Bar AutoCalculate Feature

Using a feature that Excel calls , you can view the sum of a column of cells simply by selecting the cells and looking at the status bar. The values in the selected cells are added. You can also right-click the AutoCalculate area of the status bar and choose different formulas, such as average, minimum, maximum, and count.

This feature is useful if you want to quickly check the total for a group of cells or compute the average. It also allows you to "try out" an Excel function (discussed in Lesson 5) before actually entering it into a cell. You can also view the average, minimum, maximum, and count of a range of cells. To display something other than the sum, highlight the group of cells you want the operation performed on, right-click the status bar, and select the option you want from the shortcut menu that appears (see Figure 3.3).

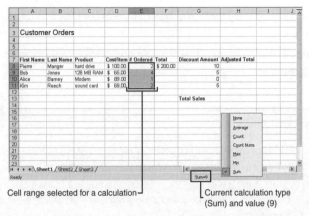

Cell range selected for a calculation

Current calculation type
(Sum) and value (9)

Figure 3.3 You can view the results of different built-in formulas in the status bar.

Timesaver tip

Missing Status Bar? If the status bar is not visible on your screen, you can display it by selecting the **View** menu and then selecting **Status Bar**.

→ Displaying Formulas

Normally, Excel does not display the formula in a cell. Instead, it displays the result of the calculation. You can view the formula by selecting the cell and looking in the Formula bar. However, if you're trying to review all the formulas in a large worksheet, it would be easier if you could see them all at once (and even print them). If you want to view formulas in a worksheet, follow these steps:

1 Open the **Tools** menu and choose **Options**.

2 Click the **View** tab.

3 In the Window options area of the View tab (near the bottom of the tab), click to select the **Formulas** check box.

4 Click **OK**.

→ Editing Formulas

Editing a formula is the same as editing any entry in Excel. The following steps show how you do it:

1 Select the cell that contains the formula you want to edit.

2 Click in the Formula bar to place the insertion point in the formula, or press **F2** to enter Edit mode (the insertion point is placed at the end of the entry in that cell).

Timesaver tip

In-Cell Editing To quickly edit the contents of a cell, double-click the cell. The insertion point appears inside the cell, and you can make any necessary changes.

3 Press the left-arrow key or the right-arrow key to move the insertion point within the formula. Then, use the **Backspace** key to delete characters to the left, or use the **Delete** key to delete characters to the right. Type any additional characters.

4 When you finish editing the data, click the **Enter** button on the Formula bar or press **Enter** to accept your changes.

4 Manipulating Formulas and Understanding Cell References

In this lesson, you learn how to copy formulas, use relative and absolute cell references, and change calculation settings.

→ Copying Formulas

Copying labels and values in Excel is no big deal. You can use the Copy and Paste commands (discussed in Lesson 8, "Editing Worksheets") or you can use some of the Fill features discussed in Lesson 2, "Entering Data into the Worksheet." Copying or moving formulas, however, is a little trickier.

Suppose that you create the formula =D8*E8 and place it into cell F8, as shown in Figure 4.1. You have designed the formula to reference cells D8 and E8. However, Excel looks at these cell references a little differently. Excel sees cell D8 as the entry that is located two cells to the left of F8 (where the formula has been placed, in this example). It sees cell E8 as being the location that is one cell to the left of F8.

Excel's method of referencing cells is called *relative referencing*. The great thing about this method of referencing cells is that when you copy a formula to a new location, it adjusts to the relative cell references around it and provides you with the correct calculation.

For example, you could copy the formula in cell F8 to cell F9, and Excel would use relative referencing to change the cell addresses in the formula. The original formula =D8*E8 would appear as D9*E9 when copied to cell F9.

Relative referencing is very useful in most situations where you copy a formula to several cells in the same column. However, it can get you into trouble when you cut and paste a formula to a new location or copy the formula to a location where it can no longer reference the appropriate cells to provide you with the correct calculation. In these situations, you must use absolute referencing so that the formula references only specified cells and does not change the cell references in the formula when pasted to the new location. Absolute referencing is discussed in the next section.

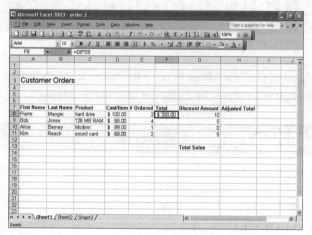

Figure 4.1 Formulas you place in Excel use relative referencing for calculations.

You can copy formulas using the Copy and Paste commands (see Lesson 8); however, when you need to copy a formula to multiple locations, you can also use the Fill feature discussed in Lesson 2.

Because Excel uses relative referencing by default, the formula adjusts to each of its new locations. An alternative way to "copy" a formula to multiple adjacent cells is to select all cells that will contain the formula before you actually write the formula in the first cell. Follow these steps:

1 Select all the cells that will contain the formula (dragging so that the cell that you will write the formula in is the first of the selected group of cells).

2 Enter the formula into the first cell.

3 Press **Ctrl+Enter** and the formula is placed in all the selected cells.

4

→ Using Relative and Absolute Cell Addresses

As mentioned at the beginning of this lesson, when you copy a formula from one place in the worksheet to another, Excel adjusts the cell references in the formulas relative to their new positions in the worksheet. There might be occasions when you don't want Excel to change the reference related to a particular cell that appears in a formula (or in an Excel function, which is discussed in Lesson 5, "Performing Calculations with Functions").

For example, suppose you have a worksheet that computes the commission made on sales by each of your salespeople. Sales have been so good that you've decided to give each person on the sales team a $200 bonus. Figure 4.2 shows the worksheet that you've created.

Notice that the bonus amount is contained in only one cell on the worksheet (cell E15). Therefore, when you create the formula used in F6 and then copied to cells F7 through F11, you need to make sure that the bonus amount in cell E15 is always referenced by the formula. This is a case where you must "absolutely" reference the bonus amount in cell E15.

$ character makes cell reference absolute

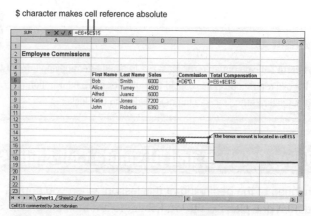

Figure 4.2 Some formulas require absolute references.

To make a cell reference in a formula absolute, add a $ (dollar sign) before the column letter and before the row number that make up the cell address. For example, in Figure 4.2, the formula in F6 must read as follows:

=E6+E15

The address, E15, refers to cell E15, meaning that cell E15 is absolutely referenced by the formula. This cell reference remains "locked" even when you copy the formula to the other cells in the E column.

To create an absolute reference in a formula (or a function, which is discussed in Lesson 5), create your formula as you normally would (as detailed in Lesson 3, "Performing Simple Calculations"). After typing or pointing out a cell address in a formula that needs to be an absolute reference, press **F4**. A dollar sign ($) is placed before the cell and row designation for that cell. Once data is labeled as absolute, you will find that if you move the data to a different cell (or cells), the formula will update itself to reference the new location.

Some formulas might contain cell addresses where you will make the column designation absolute, but not the row (or vice versa). For example, you could have a formula $A6/2. You are telling Excel that the values will always be contained in column A (it is absolute), but the row reference (6) can change when the formula is copied. Having a cell address in a formula that contains an absolute designation and a relative reference is called a *mixed reference*.

Jargon buster

Mixed References A reference that is only partially absolute, such as A$2 or $A2. When a formula that uses a mixed reference is copied to another cell, only part of the cell reference (the relative part) is adjusted.

Absolute referencing and mixed references are also required by some of Excel's built-in functions. You work with functions in the next lesson.

→ Recalculating the Worksheet

Excel automatically recalculates the results in your worksheet every time you enter a new value or edit a value or formula. This is fine for most workbooks. However, if you have a computer with limited memory and processing power, you might find that having Excel recalculate all the results in a very large worksheet every time you make a change means that you are sitting and waiting for Excel to complete the recalculation.

You can turn off the automatic recalculation. However, this won't be necessary except in situations where you are working with huge workbooks that contain a very large number of formulas, functions, and data. Turning off the automatic calculation feature also means that you must remember to manually recalculate the values in the worksheet before you print. To change the recalculation setting, take the following steps:

1 Open the **Tools** menu and choose **Options**.

2 Click the **Calculation** tab to display the options shown in Figure 4.3.

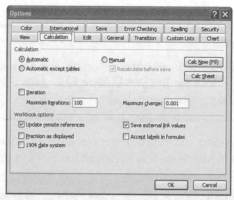

Figure 4.3 You can turn off the automatic recalculation feature.

3 Select one of the following Calculation options:

- **Automatic**—This is the default setting. It recalculates the entire workbook each time you edit or enter a formula.

- **Automatic Except Tables**—This automatically recalculates everything except formulas in a data table (data tables are used to provide a range of data for one formula and function and are used for an advanced Excel feature called "What If Analysis").

- **Manual**—This option tells Excel to recalculate only when you say so. To recalculate manually, press the **F9** key. When this option is selected, you can turn the Recalculate Before Save option off or on.

4 Click **OK**.

5 Performing Calculations with Functions

In this lesson, you learn how to perform calculations with functions and how to use the Insert Function feature to quickly insert functions into your worksheets.

→ What Are Functions?

You already learned in Lesson 3, "Performing Simple Calculations," how to create your own formulas in Excel. When you work with more complex calculations, you are better off using Excel's built-in formulas—functions.

Functions are ready-made formulas that perform a series of operations on a specified range of values. For example, to determine the sum of a series of numbers in cells A1 through H1, you can enter the function =SUM(A1:H1). Excel functions can do all kinds of calculations for all kinds of purposes, including financial and statistical calculations.

Every function consists of the following three elements:

- The = sign, which indicates that what follows is a function (formula).
- The function name, such as SUM, that indicates which operation will be performed.
- A list of cell addresses, such as (A1:H1), which are to be acted upon by the function. Some functions can include more than one set of cell addresses, which are separated by commas (such as A1,B1,H1).

You can enter functions into the worksheet by typing the function and cell references (as you did with your own formulas), or you can use the Insert Function feature, which walks you through the process of creating a function in a worksheet (you will work with the Insert Function feature in a moment). Table 5.1 lists some of the Excel functions that you will probably use most often in your worksheets.

Timesaver tip

How Ranges Are Designated When a range of cells (a contiguous group of cells) is referenced in Excel, the format A1:H1 is used. This tells you that the range of cells starts at A1 and includes all the cells from A1 to (:) and including cell H1. We look at cell ranges in more detail in Lesson 11, "Working with Ranges."

Table 5.1 Commonly Used Excel Functions

Function	Example	Description
AVERAGE	=AVERAGE(B4:B9)	Calculates the mean or average of a group of cell values.
COUNT	=COUNT(A3:A7)	Counts the number of cells that hold values in the selected range or group of cells. This can also be used to tell you how many cells are in a particular column, which tells you how many rows are in your spreadsheet.
IF	=IF(A3>=1000, "BONUS","NO BONUS")	Allows you to place a conditional function in a cell. In this example, if A3 is greater than or equal to 1000, the true value, BONUS, is used. If A3 is less than 1000, the false value, NO BONUS, is placed in the cell.
MAX	=MAX(B4:B10)	Returns the maximum value in a range of cells.
MIN	=MIN(B4:B10)	Returns the minimum value in a range of cells.
PMT	=PMT(.0825/12,360,180000)	Calculates the monthly payment on a 30-year loan (360 monthly payments) at 8.25% a year (.0825/12 a month) for $180,000.
SUM	=SUM(A1:A10)	Calculates the total in a range of cells.

> ## Timesaver tip
>
> **Specify Text with Quotation Marks** When you are entering text into a function, the text must be enclosed within quotation marks. For example, in the function =IF(A5>2000,"BONUS","NO BONUS"), if the condition is met (the cell value is greater than 2000), the word BONUS will be returned by the function. If the condition is not met, the phrase NO BONUS will be returned in the cell by the function.

Excel provides a large number of functions listed by category. There are Financial functions, Date and Time functions, Statistical functions, and Logical functions (such as the IF function described in Table 5.1). The group of functions that you use most often depends on the type of worksheets you typically build. For example, if you do a lot of accounting work, you will find that the Financial functions offer functions for computing monthly payments, figuring out the growth on an investment, and even computing the depreciation on capital equipment.

Although some commonly used functions have been defined in Table 5.1, as you become more adept at using Excel you might want to explore some of the other functions available. Select **Help**, **Microsoft Excel Help**. On the Contents tab of the Help window, open the **Function Reference** topic. Several subtopics related to Excel functions and their uses are provided.

Using AutoSum

Adding a group of cells is probably one of the most often-used calculations in an Excel worksheet. Because of this fact, Excel makes it very easy for you to place the SUM function into a cell. Excel provides the AutoSum button on the Standard toolbar. AutoSum looks at a column or row of cell values and tries to select the cells that should be included in the SUM function.

To use AutoSum, follow these steps:

1 Select the cell where you want to place the SUM function. Typically, you will choose a cell that is at the bottom of a column of values or at the end of a row of data. This makes it easy for AutoSum to figure out the range of cells that it should include in the SUM function.

2 Click the **AutoSum** button on the Standard toolbar. AutoSum inserts =SUM and the cell addresses that it thinks should be included in the function (see Figure 5.1).

3 If the range of cell addresses that AutoSum selected is incorrect, use the mouse to drag and select the appropriate group of cells.

4 Press the **Enter** key. AutoSum calculates the total for the selected range of cells.

Timesaver tip

Quick AutoSum To bypass the step where Excel displays the SUM formula and its arguments in the cell, select the cell in which you want the sum inserted and double-click the **AutoSum** button on the Standard toolbar.

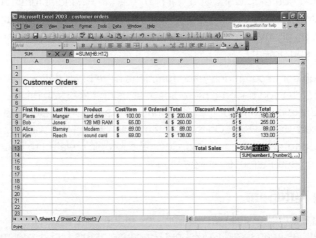

Figure 5.1 AutoSum inserts the SUM function and selects the cells that will be totaled by the function.

→ Using the Insert Function Feature

After you become familiar with a function or a group of functions, you place a particular function in an Excel worksheet by typing the function name and the cells to be referenced by the function (the same as you have done for formulas that you create as outlined in Lesson 3). However, when you are first starting out with functions, you will find it much easier to create them using the Insert Function feature. The Insert Function feature leads you through the process of inserting a function and specifying the appropriate cell addresses in the function.

For example, suppose you want to compute the average, maximum, and minimum of a group of cells that contain the weekly commissions for your sales force. Figure 5.2 shows how these three functions would look on a worksheet (the display has been changed in Excel to show you the functions rather than their results). You could use the Insert Function feature to create any or all of these functions.

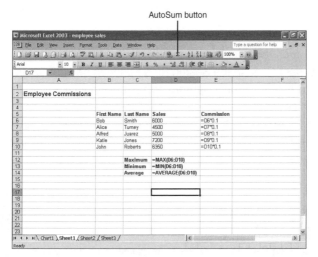

Figure 5.2 Functions such as Average, MIN, and MAX can be placed into a worksheet using the Insert Function feature.

To use the Insert Function feature, follow these steps:

1 Click in the cell where you want to place the function.

2 Click the arrow button next to the **AutoSum** button and select **More Functions**. The Insert Function dialog box appears (see Figure 5.3).

Figure 5.3 The Insert Function dialog box helps you select the function you want to use.

3 To search for a particular function, type a brief description of what you want to do in the Search for a Function box (for example, you could type **monthly payment** and Excel would show you financial functions that help you calculate monthly payments), and then click Go to conduct the search. You also can select a function category, such as Financial or Statistical, using the Select a Category drop-down box. In either case, a list of functions is provided in the Select a Function dialog box.

Jargon buster

Recently Used Functions The Insert Function dialog box by default lists the functions that you have used most recently.

4 From the Functions list, select the function you want to insert. Then click **OK**. The Function Arguments dialog box appears. This dialog box allows you to specify the range of cells (some functions require multiple ranges of cells) that the function acts upon (see Figure 5.4).

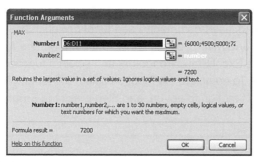

Figure 5.4 The Function Arguments dialog box is where you specify the cells that will be acted upon by the function.

5 Next, you must enter the range of cells that will be acted upon by the function. Click the **Collapse** button on the far right of the Number1 text box in the Function Arguments dialog box. This returns you to the worksheet.

6 Use the mouse to select the cells that you want to place in the function (see Figure 5.5). Then click the **Expand** button on the right of the Function Arguments dialog box.

7 Click **OK**. Excel inserts the function and cell addresses for the function into the selected cell and displays the result.

If you find that you would like to edit the list of cells acted upon by a particular function, select the cell that holds the function and click the **Insert Function** button on the Formula bar. The Function Arguments dialog box for the function appears. Select a new range of cells for the function, as discussed in steps 4 and 5.

MAX	▼ X √ fx	=MAX(D6:D10)						
	A	B	C	D	E	F	G	H	I
1								
2	Employee Commissions			Function Arguments				
3				D6:D10				
4								
5		First Name	Last Name	Sales	Commission			
6		Bob	Smith	6000	600			
7		Alice	Turney	4500	450			
8		Alfred	Juarez	5000	500			
9		Katie	Jones	7200	720			
10		John	Roberts	6350	635			
11								
12			Maximum	=MAX(D6:D10)				
13			Minimum					
14			Average					

Figure 5.5 The Function Arguments dialog box collapses and allows you to select the cells that will be acted upon by the function.

Excel 2003 also makes it easy for you to bypass the Insert Function dialog box and insert commonly used functions such as Average, Count, Max, and Min. Click the arrow to the right of the AutoSum button on the Excel Standard toolbar and select a function from the list provided. To complete the function select the range of cells that you want the function to act on, and then press the **Enter** key.

Jargon buster

What's This Function? If you'd like to know more about a particular function, click the **Help on This Function** link at the bottom of the Function Arguments dialog box. The Help window will open with help on this specific function.

6 Getting Around in Excel

In this lesson, you learn the basics of moving around in a worksheet and within a workbook.

→ Moving from Worksheet to Worksheet

Now that you've taken a look at how to enter labels, values, formulas, and functions, you should take a look at how to navigate the space provided by Excel workbooks and worksheets. By default, each workbook starts off with three worksheets. You can add or delete worksheets from the workbook as needed. Because each workbook consists of one or more worksheets, you need a way of moving easily from worksheet to worksheet. Use one of the following methods:

■ Click the tab of the worksheet you want to go to (see Figure 6.1). If the tab is not shown, use the tab scroll buttons to bring the tab into view, and then click the tab.

■ Press **Ctrl+PgDn** to move to the next worksheet or **Ctrl+PgUp** to move to the previous one.

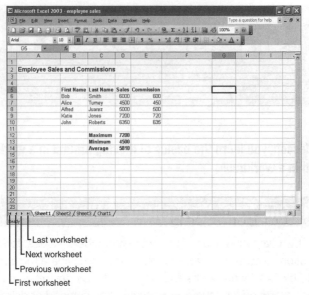

Last worksheet
Next worksheet
Previous worksheet
First worksheet

Figure 6.1 Use the tabs to move from worksheet to worksheet.

→ Switching Between Workbooks

Switching between the different workbooks that you have opened on the Windows desktop is very straightforward. By default, each workbook has its own button on the Windows taskbar and opens in its own Excel application window. To switch between workbooks, click the button for the workbook you want.

If you don't want to have a separate taskbar entry for each open Excel workbook, you can turn this feature off using the Windows in Taskbar option on the View tab of the Options dialog box (click **Tools**, **Options**). Keep in mind, however, that disabling this feature means that you will have to use the Window menu to switch between Excel workbooks. To do so, select the Window menu, and then select the name of the workbook you want to make the current workbook in the Excel application window.

→ Moving Within a Worksheet

To enter your worksheet data, you need some way of moving to the various cells within the worksheet. Keep in mind that the part of the worksheet displayed onscreen is only a small piece of the actual worksheet.

Using the Keyboard

To move around the worksheet with your keyboard, use the key combinations listed in Table 6.1.

6

Table 6.1 Moving Around a Worksheet with the Keyboard

To Move	Press This
Up one cell	Up-arrow key
Down one cell	Down-arrow key
Right one cell	Right-arrow key
Left one cell	Left-arrow key
Up one screen	Page Up
Down one screen	Page Down
Leftmost cell in a row (column A)	Home
Lower-right corner of the data area	Ctrl+End
Cell A1	Ctrl+Home
Last occupied cell to the right of a row	End+right-arrow key

You can also quickly go to a specific cell address in a worksheet using the Go To feature. Press **Ctrl+G** (or select **Edit**, **Go To**). Type the cell address you want to go to into the Reference box, and then click the **OK** button (see Figure 6.2).

Figure 6.2 The Go To feature can be used to move to a specific cell address on the worksheet.

The Go To feature keeps a list of cells that you have recently moved to using the Go To feature. To quickly move to a particular cell in the Go To list, double-click that cell address.

Timesaver tip

Even Faster Than Go To To move quickly to a specific cell on a worksheet, type the cell's address (the column letter and row number; for example, **C25**) into the Name box at the left end of the Formula bar and press **Enter**.

Using a Mouse

To scroll through a worksheet with a mouse, follow the techniques listed in Table 6.2.

Table 6.2 Moving Around a Worksheet with the Mouse

To Move	Click This
Move the selector to a particular cell	Any cell
View one more row, up or down	Up or down arrows on the vertical scrollbar
View one more column, left or right	Left or right arrows on the horizontal scrollbar
Move through a worksheet quickly	The vertical or horizontal scrollbar; drag it up or down or right and left, respectively (as you drag, a ScreenTip displays the current row/column number)

Timesaver tip

Watch the Scroll Box The size of the scroll box changes to represent the amount of the total worksheet that is currently visible. If the scroll box is large, you know you're seeing almost all of the current worksheet in the window. If the scroll box is small, most of the worksheet is currently hidden from view.

Using a Wheel-Enabled Mouse

If you use a wheel-enabled mouse (like the Microsoft IntelliMouse), you can move through a worksheet even faster than you can by using the scrollbars and a conventional mouse. Table 6.3 shows how.

Table 6.3 Moving Around a Worksheet with a Wheel-Enabled Mouse

To:	Do This:
Scroll a few rows (scroll up and down)	Rotate the wheel in the middle of the mouse forward or backward.
Scroll faster (pan)	Click and hold the wheel button, and then drag the mouse in the direction in which you want to pan. The farther away from the origin mark (the four-headed arrow) you drag the mouse, the faster the panning action. To slow the pan, drag the mouse back toward the origin mark.
Pan without holding	Click the wheel once, and then move the mouse in the wheel the direction in which you want to pan. (You'll continue to pan when you move the mouse until you turn panning off by clicking the wheel again.)
Zoom in and out	Press the **Ctrl** key as you rotate the middle wheel. If you zoom out, you can click any cell you want to jump to. You can then zoom back in so you can see your data.

7 Different Ways to View Your Worksheet

In this lesson, you learn about the various ways in which you can view your worksheets.

→ Changing the Worksheet View

Excel provides many ways to change how your worksheet appears within the Excel window. Changing the view has no effect on how your worksheets look when printed (unless you choose to hide data onscreen, a topic covered later in this lesson). However, changing the view and getting a different perspective helps you to see the overall layout of the worksheet and allows you to view worksheet cells that might not appear in the default screen view. For example, you can enlarge or reduce the size of the worksheet so that you can view more or less of it at one time.

To enlarge or reduce your view of the current worksheet, use the Zoom feature. Simply click the **Zoom** button on the Standard toolbar and select the zoom percentage you want to use from the following: 25%, 50%, 75%, 100%, or 200%. If you want to zoom by a number that's not listed, just type the number into the Zoom box and press **Enter**.

You can also have Excel zoom in on a particular portion of a worksheet. This is particularly useful when you have created very large worksheets. Select the area of the worksheet you want to zoom in on, and then click the **Zoom** button list and click **Selection**. You can then select different zoom values on the Zoom list to zoom in or out on that particular portion of the worksheet. Keep in mind that Excel zooms in on the entire worksheet, not just the selected cells. (It just makes sure that you can see the selected cells when you change the zoom values.)

You also can display your worksheet so that it takes up the full screen. This eliminates all the other items in the Excel window, such as the toolbars, the Formula bar, the status bar, and so on. Figure 7.1 shows a worksheet in the Full Screen view. To use this view, select the **View** menu and select **Full Screen**. To return to Normal view, click **Close Full Screen**.

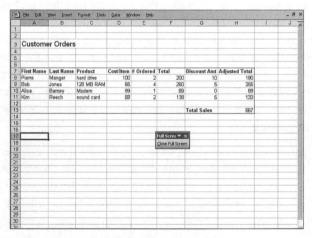

Figure 7.1 View your worksheet on the entire screen.

→ Freezing Column and Row Labels

When you work with very large worksheets, it can be very annoying as you scroll to the right or down through the worksheet when you can no longer see your row headings or column headings, respectively. For example, you might be entering customer data where the customer's name is in the first column of the worksheet, and when you scroll to the extreme right to enter data, you can no longer see the customer names.

You can freeze your column and row labels so that you can view them no matter how far you scroll down or to the right in your worksheet. For example, Figure 7.2 shows frozen column labels (columns A and B, which include the first names and last names) that allow you to see the customer names no matter how far you move to the right of the worksheet.

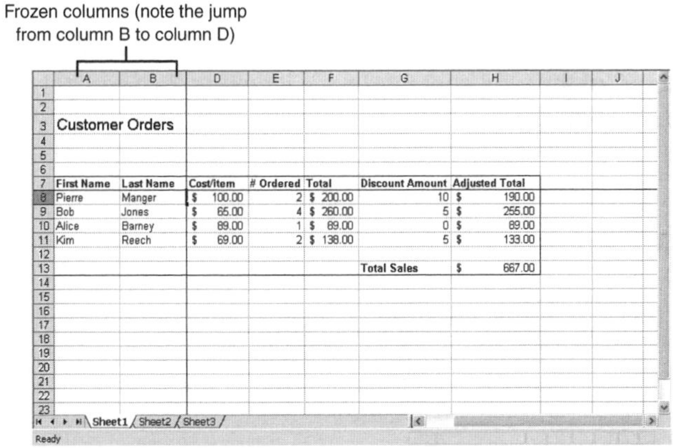

Frozen columns (note the jump from column B to column D)

	First Name	Last Name	Cost/Item	# Ordered	Total	Discount Amount	Adjusted Total

Customer Orders

First Name	Last Name	Cost/Item	# Ordered	Total	Discount Amount	Adjusted Total
Pierre	Manger	$ 100.00	2	$ 200.00	10	$ 190.00
Bob	Jones	$ 65.00	4	$ 260.00	5	$ 255.00
Alice	Barney	$ 89.00	1	$ 89.00	0	$ 89.00
Kim	Reech	$ 69.00	2	$ 138.00	5	$ 133.00
				Total Sales		$ 667.00

Figure 7.2 You can freeze row and column headings so that they remain onscreen as you scroll.

To freeze row or column headings (or both), follow these steps:

1 Click the cell to the right of the row labels and/or below any column labels you want to freeze. This highlights the cell.

2 Select the **Window** menu, and then select **Freeze Panes**.

You might want to experiment on a large worksheet. Freeze the column and row headings, and then use the keyboard or the mouse to move around in the worksheet. As you do, the row and/or column headings remain locked in their positions. This enables you to view data in other parts of the worksheet without losing track of what that data represents.

When you have finished working with the frozen column and row headings, you can easily unfreeze them. Select the **Window** menu again and select **Unfreeze Panes**.

→ Splitting Worksheets

When you work with very large worksheets, you might actually want to split the worksheet into multiple windows. This enables you to view the same worksheet in different windows. You can then scroll through the multiple copies of the same worksheet and compare data in cells that are normally far apart in the worksheet.

Figure 7.3 shows a worksheet that has been split into multiple panes. Each "copy" of the worksheet will have its own set of vertical and horizontal scrollbars.

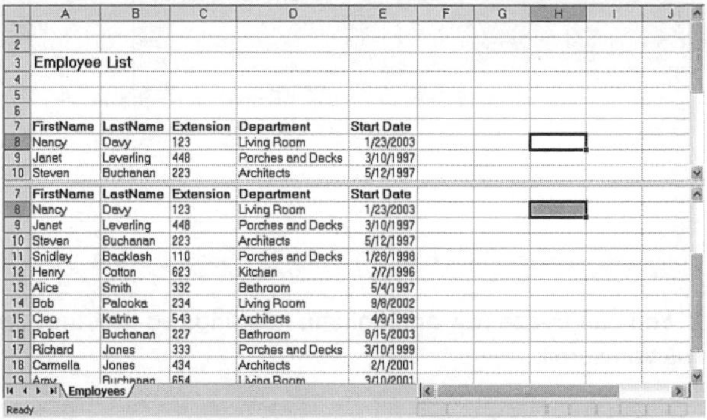

Figure 7.3 You can split a worksheet into two windows, making it easy to compare data in the worksheet.

To split a worksheet, follow these steps:

1 Click in the cell where you want to create the split. A split appears to the left of the selected cell and above the selected cell.

2 You can adjust the vertical or horizontal split bars using the mouse. Place the mouse on the split bar and drag it to a new location.

3 You can use the scrollbars in the different split panes to view data in the worksheet (different data can be viewed in each pane).

To remove the split, select the **Window** menu and select **Remove Split**.

→ Hiding Workbooks, Worksheets, Columns, and Rows

7

For those times when you're working on top-secret information (or at least information that is somewhat proprietary, such as employee salaries), you can hide workbooks, worksheets, columns, or rows from prying eyes. For example, if you have confidential data stored in one particular worksheet, you can hide that worksheet, yet still be able to view the other worksheets in that workbook. You can also hide particular columns or rows within a worksheet.

Use these methods to hide data:

■ To hide a row or a column in a worksheet, click a row or column heading to select it (you can select adjacent columns or rows by dragging across them). Then, right-click within the row or column and select **Hide** from the shortcut menu that appears. The row or column will be hidden (see Figure 7.4). To unhide the row or column, right-click the border between the hidden item and rows or columns that are visible, and then select **Unhide** from the shortcut menu.

■ To hide a worksheet, click its tab to select it. Then, open the **Format** menu and select **Sheet**, **Hide**. To unhide the worksheet, select **Format**, **Sheet**, and then **Unhide**. Select the worksheet to unhide in the Unhide dialog box that appears, and then click **OK**.

■ To hide an entire workbook, open the **Window** menu and select **Hide**. This removes the workbook from the Excel window, even though the workbook is open. To unhide the workbook, select **Window**, **Unhide**.

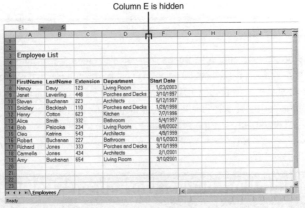

Column E is hidden

	A	B	C	D		F	G	H	I	J	K
1											
2											
3	Employee List										
4											
5											
6											
7	FirstName	LastName	Extension	Department		Start Date					
8	Nancy	Davy	123	Living Room		1/23/2003					
9	Janet	Levering	448	Porches and Decks		3/10/1997					
10	Steven	Buchanan	223	Architects		5/12/1997					
11	Snidley	Backlash	110	Porches and Decks		1/28/1998					
12	Henry	Cotton	623	Kitchen		7/7/1996					
13	Alice	Smith	332	Bathroom		5/4/1997					
14	Bob	Palooka	234	Living Room		9/8/2002					
15	Cleo	Katrina	543	Architects		4/9/1999					
16	Robert	Buchanan	227	Bathroom		8/15/2003					
17	Richard	Jones	333	Porches and Decks		3/10/1999					
18	Carmella	Jones	434	Architects		2/1/2001					
19	Amy	Buchanan	654	Living Room		3/10/2001					
20											
21											
22											
23											

Figure 7.4 Column E, which contains employee salaries, has been hidden on a worksheet.

→ Locking Cells in a Worksheet

In some situations, you might create a worksheet or worksheets and someone else will enter the data. In these situations, you might want to lock cells that contain formulas and functions so that the person doing the data entry does not accidentally overwrite or delete the worksheet formulas or functions. Locking cells in a worksheet is a two-step process. You must first select and lock the cells. Then, you must turn on protection on the entire worksheet for the "lock" to go into effect.

Follow these steps to lock cells on a worksheet:

1 Select the cells in the worksheet that you want to lock. These are typically the cells that contain formulas or functions.

2 Select **Format** and then **Cells**. The Format Cells dialog box appears. Click the **Protection** tab on the dialog box (see Figure 7.5).

3 Be sure the Locked check box is selected on the Protection tab. Then click **OK**.

4 Now you must protect the entire worksheet to have the lock feature protect the cells that you selected. Select the **Tools** menu, point at **Protections**, and then select **Protect Sheet**. The Protect Sheet dialog box appears (see Figure 7.6).

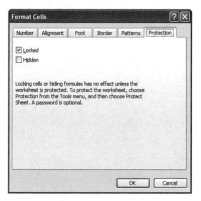

Figure 7.5 Cells can be locked using the Protection tab of the Format Cells dialog box.

Figure 7.6 The worksheet must be protected if you want to lock cells containing formulas or functions.

5 Enter a password if you want to require a password for "unprotecting" the worksheet. Then click **OK**.

The cells that you locked in steps 1, 2, and 3 will no longer accept data entry. Every time someone tries to enter data into one of those cells, Excel displays a message stating that data will not be accepted. The cells are now protected, and you can pass the workbook on to the person who handles the data entry.

8 Editing Worksheets

In this lesson, you learn how to change data and how to undo those changes if necessary. You also learn how to search for data and replace it with other data, how to spell check your work, and how to copy, move, and delete data.

→ Correcting Data

You've taken a look at entering text, values, formulas, and functions. There will definitely be occasions when you need to edit information in a cell. One way to change an entry in a cell is to replace it by selecting the cell and then entering new data. Just press **Enter** after entering the information. If you just want to modify the existing cell content, you can also edit data within a cell.

To edit information in a cell, follow these steps:

1 Select the cell in which you want to edit data.

2 To begin editing, click in the Formula bar to place the insertion point into the cell entry. To edit within the cell itself, press **F2** or double-click the cell. This puts you in Edit mode; the word Edit appears in the status bar.

3 Press the right- or left-arrow key to move the insertion point within the entry. Press the **Backspace** key to delete characters to the left of the insertion point; press the **Delete** key to delete characters to the right. Then, type any characters you want to add.

4 Press the **Enter** key when you have finished making your changes.

If you change your mind and you no longer want to edit your entry, click the **Cancel** button on the Formula bar or press **Esc**.

Timesaver tip

Moving to the Beginning or End of a Cell Entry In Edit mode, you can quickly move to the beginning or end of a cell's contents. Press **Home** to move to the beginning of the entry; press **End** to move to the end of the entry.

→ Undoing an Action

Although editing a worksheet is supposed to improve it, you might find that you've done something to a cell or range of cells that you had not intended. This is where the Undo feature comes in.

 You can undo just about any action while working in Excel, including any changes you make to a cell's data. To undo a change, click the **Undo** button on the Standard toolbar (or select **Edit**, **Undo**).

 You can also undo an undo. Just click the **Redo** button on the Standard toolbar.

Timesaver tip

Undoing/Redoing More Than One Thing The Undo button undoes only the most recent action. To undo several previous actions, click the **Undo** button multiple times or click the drop-down arrow on the Undo button and select the number of actions you want undone.

→ Using the Replace Feature

Suppose you've entered a particular label or value into the worksheet and find that you have consistently entered it incorrectly. A great way to change multiple occurrences of a label or value is using Excel's Replace feature; you can locate data in the worksheet and replace it with new data. To find and replace data, follow these steps:

1 Select the **Edit** menu, and then select **Replace**. The Find and Replace dialog box appears, as shown in Figure 8.1.

Figure 8.1 Find and replace data with the Find and Replace dialog box.

2 Type the text or value that you want to find into the **Find What** text box.

3 Click in the **Replace With** text box and type the text you want to use as replacement text.

4 To expand the options available to you in the dialog box, click the **Options** button (Figure 8.1 shows the dialog box in its expanded form).

5 If you want to match the exact case of your entry so that Excel factors in capitalization, click the **Match Case** check box. If you want to locate cells that contain exactly what you entered into the Find What text box (and no additional data), click the **Match Entire Cell Contents** check box.

6 To search for entries with particular formatting, click the **Format** button on the right of the Find What box. The Find Format dialog box appears (see Figure 8.2). You can search for entries that have been assigned number, alignment, font, border, patterns, or protection using the appropriate tab on the Find Format dialog box. After making your selection, click the **OK** button.

7 You can also replace your entries with a particular formatting. Click the **Format** button on the right of the Replace With box. The Replace Format dialog box appears. It is the same as the Find Format dialog box. Simply select any formats you want to assign to your replacement, and then click **OK**.

8 Click **Find Next** to find the first occurrence of your specified entry.

Figure 8.2 The Find Format dialog box enables you to search for entries that have been assigned a particular formatting.

9 When an occurrence is found, it is highlighted. Click **Replace** to replace only this occurrence and then click **Find Next** to find the next occurrence.

10 If you want to find all the occurrences, click **Find All**; you can also replace all the occurrences of the entry with **Replace All**.

11 When you have finished working with the Find and Replace dialog boxclick **Close**.

Timesaver tip

Search an Entire Workbook If you want to search an entire workbook for a particular entry, click the **Within** drop-down list in the Find and Replace dialog box and select **Workbook**.

If you don't need to replace an entry but would like to find it in the worksheet, you can use the Find feature. Select **Edit**, **Find**, and then type the data you want to locate into the Find What text box and click **Find Next**.

→ Checking Your Spelling

Because worksheets also include text entries, you might want to make sure that you check for any misspellings in a worksheet before printing the data. Excel offers a spell-checking feature that finds and corrects misspellings in a worksheet.

To run the Spelling Checker, follow these steps:

1 Click the **Spelling** button on the Standard toolbar (or select **Tools, Spelling**). The Spelling dialog box appears. Excel finds the first misspelled word and displays it at the top of the Spelling dialog box. A suggested correction appears in the Suggestions box (see Figure 8.3).

8

Figure 8.3 Correct spelling mistakes with the options in the Spelling dialog box.

2 To accept the suggestion in the Suggestions box, click **Change**, or click **Change All** to change all occurrences of the misspelled word.

3 If the suggestion in the Suggestions box is not correct, you can do any of the following:

- Select a different suggestion from the Suggestions box, and then click **Change** or **Change All**.

- Type your own correction into the Change To box, and then click **Change** or **Change All**.

- Click **Ignore Once** to leave the word unchanged.

- Click **Ignore All** to leave all occurrences of the word unchanged.

- Click **Add to Dictionary** to add the word to the dictionary so that Excel won't flag it as misspelled again.

- Click **AutoCorrect** to add a correctly spelled word to the AutoCorrect list so that Excel can correct it automatically as you type.

  - If you make a mistake related to a particular entry, click the **Undo Last** button to undo the last change that you made.

4 You might see a message asking whether you want to continue checking spelling at the beginning of the sheet. If so, click **Yes** to continue. When the Spelling Checker can't find any more misspelled words, it displays a prompt telling you that the spelling check is complete. Click **OK** to confirm that the spelling check is finished.

Timesaver tip

Setting Spelling Options If you want to set options related to the Spelling feature, such as ignoring words in uppercase and words with numbers, click the **Options** button in the Spelling dialog box. This takes you to the Options dialog box for the Spelling Checker. Set options as needed and then click **OK** to return to the Spelling dialog box.

→ Copying and Moving Data

In Lesson 2, you learned how to use the Fill feature to copy a particular entry to multiple cells. In this section, you take a closer look at the Copy feature. When you copy or cut data in a cell, that data is held in a temporary storage area (a part of the computer's memory) called the Clipboard.

Excel 2003 (and all the Office 2003 applications) makes it easy for you to work with the Clipboard because it can be viewed in the Office Clipboard task pane (you look at the Clipboard later in this lesson). This enables you to keep track of items that you have copied or cut to the Clipboard. The Clipboard not only enables you to copy or move data with Excel, but it enables you to place Excel data directly into another application.

When you copy data, you create a duplicate of data in a cell or range of cells. Follow these steps to copy data:

1 Select the cell(s) that you want to copy. You can select any range or several ranges if you want. (See Lesson 11, "Working with Ranges," for more information).

2 Click the **Copy** button on the Standard toolbar. The contents of the selected cell(s) are copied to the Clipboard.

8

3 Select the first cell in the area where you would like to place the copy. (To copy the data to another worksheet or workbook, change to that worksheet or workbook first.)

4 Click the **Paste** button. Excel inserts the contents of the Clipboard at the location of the insertion point.

You can copy the same data to several places by repeating the **Paste** command. Items remain on the Clipboard until you remove them.

Using Drag and Drop

The fastest way to copy something is to drag and drop it. Select the cells you want to copy, hold down the **Ctrl** key, and drag the border of the range you selected (see Figure 8.4). When you release the mouse button, the contents are copied to the new location. To insert the data between existing cells, press **Ctrl+Shift** as you drag.

To drag a copy to a different sheet, press **Ctrl+Alt** as you drag the selection to the sheet's tab. Excel switches you to that sheet, where you can drop your selection into the appropriate location.

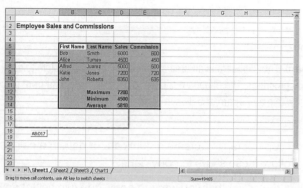

Figure 8.4 Dragging is the fastest way to copy data.

Moving Data

Moving data is similar to copying except that the data is removed from its original place and placed into the new location.

To move data, follow these steps:

1 Select the cells you want to move.

2 Click the **Cut** button.

3 Select the first cell in the area where you want to place the data. To move the data to another worksheet, change to that worksheet.

4 Click **Paste**.

Using Drag and Drop to Move Data

You can also move data using drag and drop. Select the data to be moved, and then drag the border of the selected cells to its new location. To insert the data between existing cells, press **Shift** while you drag. To move the data to a different worksheet, press the **Alt** key and drag the selection to the worksheet's tab. You're switched to that sheet, where you can drop your selection at the appropriate point.

→ Using the Office Clipboard

You can use the Office Clipboard to store multiple items that you cut or copy from an Excel worksheet (or workbook). You can then paste or move these items within Excel or to other Office applications. The Office Clipboard can hold up to 24 items.

Important

What a Drag! You can't use the drag-and-drop feature to copy or move data to the Office Clipboard.

The Office Clipboard is viewed in the Clipboard task pane. Follow these steps to open the Office Clipboard:

1 Select the **Edit** menu, and then select **Office Clipboard**. The Clipboard task pane appears. Any items that you have cut or copied appear on the Clipboard (see Figure 8.5).

Figure 8.5 The Clipboard provides a list of items that you have cut or copied.

2 To paste an item that appears on the Clipboard, click in a cell on the worksheet, and then click the item on the Clipboard. It is then pasted into the selected cell.

You can remove any of the items from the Clipboard. Place the mouse pointer on an item listed on the Clipboard and click the drop-down arrow that appears. Click **Delete** on the shortcut menu that appears.

You can also clear all the items from the Clipboard. Click the **Clear All** button at the top of the Clipboard task pane.

Timesaver tip

Open the Clipboard from the System Tray You can quickly open the Office Clipboard in any Office application by double-clicking the Clipboard icon in the Windows System Tray (at the far right of the Windows taskbar).

→ Deleting Data

To delete the data in a cell or range of cells, select them and press **Delete**. Excel also offers some additional options for deleting cells and their contents:

- With the **Edit**, **Clear** command, you can delete only the formatting of a cell (or an attached comment) without deleting its contents. The formatting of a cell includes the cell's color, border style, numeric format, font size, and so on. You'll learn more about this option in a moment.

- With the **Edit**, **Delete** command, you can remove cells and then shift surrounding cells over to take their place (this option is described in more detail in Lesson 12, "Inserting and Removing Cells, Rows, and Columns").

To use the Clear command to remove the formatting of a cell or a note, follow these steps:

1 Select the cells you want to clear.

2 Open the **Edit** menu and point at **Clear**. The Clear submenu appears.

3 Select the desired Clear option: **All** (which clears the cells of all contents, formatting, and notes), **Formats**, **Contents**, or **Comments**.

9 Changing How Numbers and Text Look

In this lesson, you learn how to customize the appearance of numbers in your worksheet and how to customize your text formatting to achieve the look you want.

→ Formatting Text and Numbers

When you work in Excel, you work with two types of formatting: value formatting and font formatting. In value formatting, you assign a particular number style to a cell (or cells) that holds numeric data. You can assign a currency style, a percent style, or one of several other numeric styles to values.

Another formatting option available to you in Excel relates to different font attributes. For example, you can add bold or italic to the contents of a cell or cells. You can also change the font used for a range of cells or increase the font size.

Next, you take a look at numeric formatting, and then you look at how different font attributes are controlled in Excel.

→ Using the Style Buttons to Format Numbers

The Formatting toolbar (just below the Standard toolbar) contains several buttons for applying a format to your numbers, including the following:

Button	Name	Example/Description
$	Currency Style	$1,200.90
%	Percent Style	20.90%
,	Comma Style	1,200.90
.0 .00	Increase Decimal	Adds one decimal place
.00 .0	Decrease Decimal	Deletes one decimal place

To use one of these buttons, select the cell or cells you want to format, and then click the desired button. If you would like more formatting options for numeric values, read on; they are covered in the next section.

→ Numeric Formatting Options

The numeric values that you place in your Excel cells are more than just numbers; they often represent dollar amounts, a date, or a percentage. If the various numeric style buttons on the Formatting toolbar (discussed in the previous section) do not offer the exact format you want for your numbers, don't worry. Excel's Format Cells dialog box offers a wide range of number formats and even allows you to create custom formats.

To use the Format Cells dialog box to assign numeric formatting to cells in a worksheet, follow these steps:

1 Select the cell or range that contains the values you want to format.

2 Select the **Format** menu and select **Cells**. The Format Cells dialog box appears.

3 Click the **Number** tab. The different categories of numeric formats are displayed in a Category list (see Figure 9.1).

4 In the Category list, select the numeric format category you want to use. The sample box displays the default format for that category.

5 Click **OK** to assign the numeric format to the selected cells.

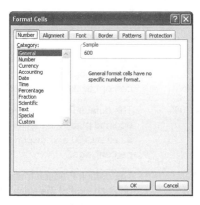

Figure 9.1 Apply a numeric format in the Number tab of the Format Cells dialog box.

As you can see from the Number tab on the Format Cells dialog box, Excel offers several numeric formatting styles. Table 9.1 provides a list of these different number formats.

9

Table 9.1 Excel's Number Formats

Number Format	Examples	Description
General	10.6 $456,908.00	Excel displays your value as you enter it. In other words, this format displays currency or percent signs only if you enter them yourself.
Number	3400.50 €120.39	The default Number format has two decimal places. Negative numbers are preceded by a minus sign, but they can also appear in red and/or parentheses.
Currency	$3,400.50 €3,400.50	The default Currency format has two decimal places and a dollar sign. Negative numbers appear with a minus sign, but they can also appear in red and/or parentheses.
Accounting	$3,400.00 $978.21	Use this format to align dollar signs and decimal points in a column. The default Accounting format has two decimal places and a dollar sign.
Date	11/7	The default Date format is the month and day separated by a slash; however, you can select from numerous other formats.

Table 9.1 continued

Number Format	Examples	Description
Time	10:00	The default Time format is the hour and minutes separated by a colon; however, you can opt to display seconds, a.m., or p.m.
Percentage	99.50%	The default Percentage format has two decimal places. Excel multiplies the value in a cell by 100 and displays the result with a percent sign.
Fraction	1/2	The default Fraction format is up to one digit on each side of the slash. Use this format to display the number of digits you want on each side of the slash and the fraction type (such as halves, quarters, eighths, and so on).
Scientific	3.40E+03	The default Scientific format has two decimal places. Use this format to display numbers in scientific notation.
Text	135RV90	Use Text format to display both text and numbers in a cell as text. Excel displays the entry exactly as you type it.
Special	02110	This format is specifically designed to display ZIP codes, phone numbers, and Social Security numbers correctly so that you don't have to enter any special characters, such as hyphens.
Custom	00.0%	Use Custom format to create your own number format. You can use any of the format codes in the Type list and then make changes to those codes. The # symbol represents a number placeholder, and 0 represents a zero placeholder.

You can also open the Format Cell dialog box using a shortcut menu. Select the cell or cells that you want to assign a numeric format to, and then right-click those cells. On the shortcut menu that appears, select **Format Cells**. Then, select the **Number** tab to select your numeric format.

Important

That's Not the Date I Entered! If you enter a date into a cell that is already formatted with the Number format, the date appears as a value that represents the number of days between January 1, 1900, and that date. Change the cell's formatting from a Number format to a Date format and select a date type. The entry in the cell then appears as an actual date.

Timesaver tip

How Do I Get Rid of a Numeric Format? To remove a number format from a cell (and return it to General format), select the cell whose formatting you want to remove, open the **Edit** menu, select **Clear**, and select **Formats**.

9

→ How You Can Make Text Look Different

When you type text into a cell, Excel automatically formats it in the Arial font with a text size of 10 points. The 12-point font size is considered typical for business documents (the higher the point size, the bigger the text is; there are approximately 72 points in an inch). You can select from several fonts (such as Baskerville, Modern, or Rockwell) and change the size of any font characters in a cell. You can also apply special font attributes, such as bold, italic, and underline.

Jargon buster

Font A font is a set of characters that have the same typeface, which means they are of a single design (such as Times New Roman).

Before you take a look at applying different font attributes to the cells in a worksheet, take a look at how you change the default font for all your Excel workbooks. This enables you to select a different font and font size for your worksheets.

To change the default font, follow these steps:

1 Select **Tools** and then click **Options** to open the Options dialog box.

2 Click the **General** tab (see Figure 9.2).

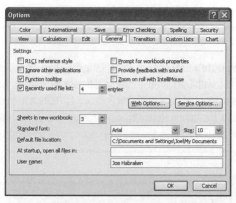

Figure 9.2 You can set a new default font and font size for your Excel workbooks.

3 In the Standard Font area, use the drop-down list to select a new font. Use the Size drop-down list to select a new default font size.

4 When you click the **OK** button, Excel makes your preference the default font and size.

→ Changing Text Attributes with Toolbar Buttons

When you are working on your various Excel worksheets, you will probably apply a variety of formatting options to the different cells in a particular worksheet. A fast way to assign text attributes, such as bold and italic, is to use the various font attribute buttons on the Excel Formatting toolbar.

To use the Formatting toolbar to change text attributes, follow these steps:

1 Select the cell or range that contains the text whose look you want to change.

2 To change the font, click the **Font** drop-down list, and select a new font name. To change the font size, click the **Font Size** drop-down list and select the size you want to use. You can also type the point size into the Font Size box and then press **Enter**.

B

I

U

3 To add an attribute such as bold, italic, or underlining to the selected cells, click the appropriate button: **Bold**, **Italic**, or **Underline**, respectively.

You can also change the color of the font in a cell or cells. Select the cell or cells and click the **Font Color** drop-down arrow on the Formatting toolbar. Select a font color from the Color palette that appears.

→ Accessing Different Font Attributes

If you would like to access a greater number of font format options for a cell or range of cells, you can use the Font tab of the Format Cells dialog box. It provides access to different fonts, font styles, font sizes, font colors, and other text attributes, such as strikethrough and superscript/subscript. To format cells using the Font tab of the Format Cells dialog box, follow these steps:

1 Select the cell or range that contains the text you want to format.

2 Select the **Format** menu and select **Cells**, or press **Ctrl+1**. (You can also right-click the selected cells and choose **Format Cells** from the shortcut menu.)

3 Click the **Font** tab. The Font tab provides drop-down lists and check boxes for selecting the various font attributes (see Figure 9.3).

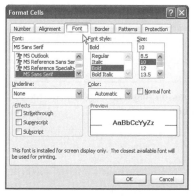

Figure 9.3 The Font tab provides access to all the font attributes.

4 Select the options you want.

5 Click **OK** to close the dialog box and return to your worksheet.

→ Aligning Text in Cells

When you enter data into a cell, that data is aligned automatically. Text is aligned on the left, and numbers are aligned on the right (values resulting from a formula or function are also right-aligned). Both text and numbers are initially set at the bottom of the cells. However, you can change both the vertical and the horizontal alignment of data in your cells.

Follow these steps to change the alignment:

1 Select the cell or range you want to align.

2 Select the **Format** menu and then select **Cells**. The Format Cells dialog box appears.

3 Click the **Alignment** tab (see Figure 9.4).

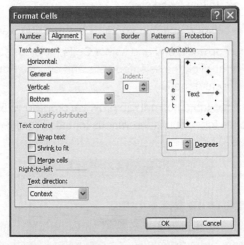

Figure 9.4 Select from the Alignment options on the Alignment tab of the Format Cells dialog box.

4 Choose from the following options to set the alignment:

- **Horizontal**—Lets you specify a left/right alignment in the cells. (The **Center Across** selection centers a title or other text within a range of cells, which is discussed in a moment.)

- **Vertical**—Lets you specify how you want the text aligned in relation to the top and bottom of the cells.

- **Orientation**—Lets you flip the text sideways or print it from top to bottom instead of left to right.

- **Wrap Text**—Tells Excel to wrap long lines of text within a cell without changing the width of the cell. (Normally, Excel displays all text in a cell on one line.)

- **Shrink to Fit**—Shrinks the text to fit within the cell's current width. If the cell's width is adjusted, the text increases or decreases in size accordingly.

- **Merge Cells**—Combines several cells into a single cell. All data is overlaid, except for the cell in the upper-left corner of the selected cells.

5 Click **OK** when you have finished making your selections.

9

Timesaver tip

Changing Text Orientation The Alignment tab also provides an Orientation box that enables you to rotate text within a cell or a group of merged cells. Drag the degree dial on the Alignment tab or use the Degree box to specify the amount of rotation for the text.

Aligning Text from the Toolbar

As with the font attributes such as bold and italic, you can also select certain alignment options directly from the Formatting toolbar. Table 9.2 lists the buttons that enable you to align the text.

Table 9.2 Alignment Buttons

Button	Name	Description
	Align Left	Places data at left edge of cell
	Align Right	Places data at right edge of cell
	Center	Centers data in cell
	Merge and Center	Centers data in selected cell range

Excel also enables you to indent your text within a cell. If you're typing a paragraph's worth of information into a single cell, for example, you can indent that paragraph by selecting **Left Alignment** from the Horizontal list box in the Format Cells dialog box (as explained earlier). After selecting Left Alignment, set the amount of indent you want with the Indent spin box in the Format Cells dialog box.

In addition, you can add an indent quickly by clicking the buttons on the Formatting toolbar, as listed in Table 9.3.

Table 9.3 Indent Buttons

Button	Name	Description
	Decrease Indent	Removes an indent or creates a negative indent
	Increase Indent	Adds an indent

Combining Cells and Wrapping Text

As shown in Table 9.2 in the last section, you can center text across a range of cells or merge several cells to hold a sheet title or other text information. If you want to center a title or other text over a range of cells, select the entire range of blank cells in which you want the text centered. This should include the cell that contains the text you want to center (which should be in the cell on the far left of the cell range). Then, click the **Merge and Center** button on the Formatting toolbar.

Combining a group of cells also allows you to place a special heading or other text into the cells (this works well in cases where you use a large font size for the text). Select the cells that you want to combine. Then, select **Format, Cells** and select the **Alignment** tab of the Format Cells dialog box.

Click the **Merge Cells** check box and then click **OK**. The cells are then merged.

If you have a cell or a group of merged cells that holds a large amount of text (such as an explanation), you might want to wrap the text within the cell or merged cells. Click the cell that holds the text entry, and then select **Format, Cells**. Select the **Alignment** tab of the Format Cells dialog box.

Click the **Wrap Text** checkbox. Then click **OK**.

→ Copying Formats with Format Painter

After applying a numeric format or various font attributes to a cell or cell range, you can easily copy those formatting options to other cells. This works whether you're copying numeric or text formatting or shading or borders, as you'll learn in upcoming lessons. To copy a format from one cell to another, follow these steps:

1 Select the cells that contain the formatting you want to copy.

2 Click the **Format Painter** button on the Standard toolbar. Excel copies the formatting. The mouse pointer changes into a paintbrush with a plus sign next to it.

3 Click one cell or drag over several cells to which you want to apply the copied formatting.

4 Release the mouse button, and Excel copies the formatting and applies it to the selected cells.

Timesaver tip

Painting Several Cells To paint several areas with the same formatting at one time, double-click the **Format Painter** button to toggle it on. When you're through, press **Esc** or click the **Format Painter** button again to return to a normal mouse pointer.

10 Adding Cell Borders and Shading

In this lesson, you learn how to add borders and shading to your worksheets.

→ Adding Borders to Cells

As you work with your worksheet onscreen, you'll notice that each cell is identified by gridlines that surround the cell. By default, these gridlines do not print; even if you choose to print them, they don't look very good on the printed page. To create well-defined lines on the printout (and onscreen, for that matter), you can add borders to selected cells or entire cell ranges. A border can appear on all four sides of a cell or only on selected sides; it's up to you.

Timesaver tip

Printing the Gridlines It's true that gridlines do not print by default. But if you want to try printing your worksheet with gridlines, just to see what it looks like, open the **File** menu, select **Page Setup**, click the **Sheet** tab, check the **Gridlines** box, and click **OK**.

To add borders to a cell or range, perform the following steps:

1 Select the cell(s) around which you want a border to appear.

2 Open the **Format** menu and choose **Cells**. The Format Cells dialog box appears.

3 Click the **Border** tab to see the Border options shown in Figure 10.1.

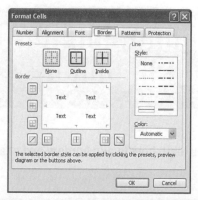

Figure 10.1 Choose Border options from the Format Cells dialog box.

4 Select the desired position, style (thickness), and color for the border. The position of the border is selected using the buttons along the left of the Border box. You can also click inside the **Border** box itself to place the border.

5 Click **OK** or press **Enter**.

When you're adding borders to a worksheet, hiding the gridlines onscreen gives you a preview of how the borders will look when printed. To hide gridlines, select the **Tools** menu, select **Options** (this opens the Options dialog box), and then select the **View** tab. Remove the check mark from the Gridlines check box, and then click **OK** to return to the worksheet. Selecting this option has no effect on whether the gridlines actually print, only on whether they are displayed onscreen.

Timesaver tip

Add Borders from the Toolbar You can use the Borders button on the Formatting toolbar to add a border to cells or cell ranges. Select the cells, and then click the **Borders** drop-down arrow on the Formatting toolbar to select a border type.

→ Adding Shading to Cells

Another way to offset certain cells in a worksheet is to add shading to those cells. With shading, you can add a color or gray shading to the background of a cell. You can add shading that consists of a solid color, or you can select a pattern as part of the shading options, such as a repeating diagonal line.

Follow these steps to add shading to a cell or range. As you make your selections, keep in mind that if you plan to print your worksheet with a black-and-white printer, the colors you select might not provide enough contrast on the printout to provide any differentiation between ranges of cells. You can always use the Print Preview command (as explained in Lesson 14, "Printing Your Workbook") to view your results in black and white before you print.

1 Select the cell(s) you want to shade.

2 Open the **Format** menu and choose **Cells**.

3 Click the **Patterns** tab. Excel displays the shading options (see Figure 10.2).

4 Click the **Pattern** drop-down arrow to see a grid that contains colors and patterns.

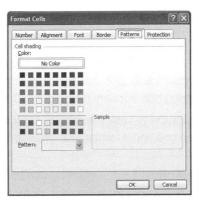

Figure 10.2 Choose colors and patterns from the Patterns tab of the Format Cells dialog box.

5 Select the shading color and pattern you want to use. The Color options let you choose a color for the overall shading. The Pattern options let you select a black or colored pattern that is placed on top of the cell-shading color you selected. A preview of the results appears in the Sample box.

6 When you have finished making your selections, click **OK**.

Timesaver tip

Add Cell Shading with the Toolbar Select the cells you want to shade. Click the **Fill Color** drop-down arrow on the Formatting toolbar and then select the fill color from the Color palette that appears.

→ Using AutoFormat

If you don't want to take the time to test different border types and shading styles, you can let Excel help you with the task of adding some emphasis and interest to the cells of your worksheet. You can take advantage of AutoFormat, which provides various predesigned table formats that you can apply to a worksheet.

To use predesigned formats, perform the following steps:

1 Select the cell(s) that contain the data you want to format. This could be the entire worksheet.

2 Select the **Format** menu, and then select **AutoFormat**. The AutoFormat dialog box appears (see Figure 10.3).

3 Scroll through the list to view the various AutoFormat styles provided. When you find a format that you want to use, click it to select it.

4 To prevent AutoFormat from overwriting certain existing formatting (such as numbers, alignment, or fonts), click the **Options** button and deselect the appropriate check boxes.

5 Click **OK** and your worksheet is formatted.

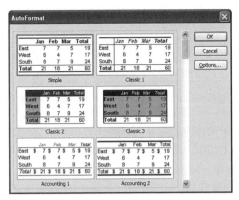

Figure 10.3 Select a format from the AutoFormat dialog box.

10

Timesaver tip

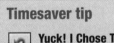 **Yuck! I Chose That?** If you don't like what AutoFormat did to your work sheet, click the **Undo** button (or press **Ctrl+Z**).

→ Applying Conditional Formatting

Another useful formatting feature that Excel provides is conditional formatting. Conditional formatting allows you to specify that certain results in the worksheet be formatted so that they stand out from the other entries in the worksheet. For example, if you wanted to track all the monthly sales figures that are below a certain amount, you can use conditional formatting to format them in red. Conditional formatting formats only cells that meet a certain condition.

To apply conditional formatting, follow these steps:

1 Select the cells to which you want to apply the conditional formatting.

2 Select the **Format** menu and select **Conditional Formatting**. The Conditional Formatting dialog box appears, as shown in Figure 10.4.

Figure 10.4 Apply formats conditionally to highlight certain values.

3 Be sure that **Cell Value Is** is selected in the Condition 1 drop-down box on the left of the dialog box.

4 In the next drop-down box to the right, you select the condition. The default is Between. Other conditions include Equal To, Greater Than, Less Than, and other possibilities. Use the drop-down box to select the appropriate condition.

5 After selecting the condition, you must specify a cell or cells in the worksheet that Excel can use as a reference for the conditional formatting. For example, if you select Less Than as the condition, you must specify a cell in the worksheet that contains a value that can be used for comparison with the cells that you are applying the conditional formatting to. Click the **Shrink** button on the Conditional Formatting dialog box. You are returned to the worksheet. Select the reference cell for the condition.

6 Click the **Expand** button on the Conditional Formatting dialog box to expand the dialog box.

7 Now you can set the formatting that will be applied to cells that meet your condition. Click the **Format** button in the Conditional Formatting dialog box and select the formatting options for your condition in the Format Cells dialog box. Then click **OK**. Figure 10.5 shows a conditional format that applies bold and italic to values that are greater than the value contained in cell F8.

8 After setting the conditions to be met for conditional formatting (you can click **Add** to set more than one condition), click **OK**.

Figure 10.5 Set the various options for your conditional formatting.

You are returned to the worksheet. Cells that meet the condition you set up for conditional formatting will be formatted with the options you specified. Figure 10.6 shows cells that the settings used in Figure 10.5 conditionally formatted.

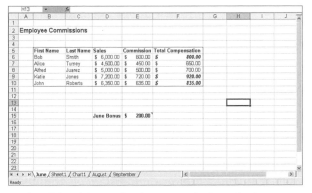

Figure 10.6 Conditional formatting formats only the cells that meet your conditions.

Timesaver tip

Conditional Formatting Applied to Formulas You can also set up conditional formatting to highlight cells that contain a particular formula or function. Select **Formula Is** for Condition 1 in the Conditional Formatting dialog box and then type the formula or function in the box to the right.

11 Working with Ranges

In this lesson, you learn how to select and name ranges.

→ What Is a Range?

When you select a group of cells (which you have done numerous times in the various Excel lessons), you are in fact selecting a range. A cell range can consist of one cell or any group of contiguous cells.

Ranges are referred to by their anchor points (the upper-left corner and the lower-right corner). For example, a range that begins with cell C10 and ends with I14 is referred to as C10:I14.

Jargon buster

Range A group of contiguous cells in an Excel worksheet.

Selecting ranges is certainly not rocket science, but you can do a number of things with a selected range of cells. For example, you can select a range of cells and print them (rather than printing the entire worksheet). You can also name ranges, which makes it much easier to include the cell range in a formula or function (you learn about range names and using range names in formulas later in this lesson). A few tricks for selecting cell ranges are discussed in the next section.

→ Selecting a Range

To select a range using the mouse, follow these steps:

1 Move the mouse pointer to the upper-left corner of a range.

2 Click and hold the left mouse button.

3 Drag the mouse to the lower-right corner of the range and release the mouse button. The cells are highlighted on the worksheet (see Figure 11.1).

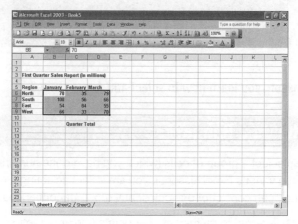

Figure 11.1 A range is any combination of cells that forms a rectangle or a square.

Techniques that you can use to quickly select a row, a column, an entire worksheet, or several ranges are shown in Table 11.1.

Table 11.1 Selection Techniques

To Select This	Do This
Several ranges	Select the first range, hold down the **Ctrl** key, and select the next range. Continue holding down the **Ctrl** key while you select additional ranges.
Row	Click the row heading number at the left edge of the worksheet. You also can press **Shift+Spacebar**. To select several adjacent rows, drag over their headers. To select nonadjacent rows, press **Ctrl** as you click each row's header.
Column	Click the column heading letter at the top edge of the worksheet. You also can press **Ctrl+Spacebar**.
Entire worksheet	Click the **Select All** button (the blank rectangle in the upper-left corner of the worksheet, above row 1 and left of column A). You also can press **Ctrl+A**.
The same range on several sheets	Press and hold **Ctrl** as you click the worksheets you want to use, and then select the range in the usual way.
Range that is out of view	Press **Ctrl+G** (**Go To**) or click in the **Name** box on the Formula bar and type the address of the range you want to select. For example, to select the range R100 to T250, type **R100:T250** and press **Enter**.

Selected cells are highlighted in a slightly grayed tone, so you can still read your data.

→ Naming Ranges

Up to this point, when you have created formulas or functions or formatted cells in a worksheet, you have specified cells and cell ranges using the cell addresses. You can also name a cell or range of cells. You could select a range of values and assign that range a name. For example, you could select a range of cells that includes your expenses and name that range EXPENSES. You can then name a range of cells that includes your income and name that range INCOME. It would be very simple to then create a formula that subtracts your expenses from your income using the range names that you created. The formula would be written as follows:

=SUM(INCOME) – SUM(EXPENSES)

You are telling Excel to add the INCOME range and add the EXPENSES range. The formula then subtracts the total EXPENSES from the total INCOME. Note that the SUM function is used along with simple subtraction in this formula to provide the desired results.

Using range names in formulas and functions can definitely make your life easier. Range names are very useful when you create formulas or functions that pull information from more than one worksheet in a workbook or different workbooks. You can even use a range name to create a chart (you learn about charts in Lesson 15, "Creating Charts").

Follow these steps to name a range:

1 Select the range you want to name (the cells must be located on the same worksheet). If you want to name a single cell, simply select that cell.

2 Select the **Insert** menu, point at **Name**, and then select **Define**. The Define Name dialog box appears (see Figure 11.2).

3 Type the name for the range in the box at the top of the dialog box. You can use up to 255 characters, and valid range names can include letters, numbers, periods, and underlines, but no spaces.

4 Click the **Add** button to name the range. The name is added to the list of range names.

5 Click **OK**.

Figure 11.2 Use the Define Name dialog box to name a cell range.

Timesaver tip

Selecting a Different Range You can change the selected range from the Define Name dialog box. Click the **Shrink** button at the bottom of the dialog box, and then select the range on the worksheet. To return to the dialog box, click the **Expand** button on the Define Name dialog box.

You can also use the Define Name dialog box to delete any unwanted range names. Select **Insert**, point at **Name**, and then select **Define**. Select an unwanted range name from the list and click the **Delete** button. To close the dialog box, click **OK**.

Timesaver tip

Quickly Create a Range Name You can also create a range name by typing it into the Name box on the Formula bar (this box normally shows the location of the selected range or cell). Select the cell range, click in the Name box, and type the name for the range. Then press **Enter**.

→ Creating Range Names from Worksheet Labels

You can also create range names using the column and row labels that you have created for your worksheet. The row labels are used to create a range name for each row of cells, and the column labels are used to create a range name for each column of cells. Follow these steps:

1 Select the worksheet, including the column and row labels.

2 Select the **Insert** menu, point at **Name**, and then select **Create**. The Create Names dialog box appears (see Figure 11.3).

Figure 11.3 Use the Create Names dialog box to create range names for the cells in the worksheet.

3 Click in the check boxes that define the position of the row and column labels in the worksheet.

4 After specifying the location of the row and column labels, click **OK**.

You can check the range names (and their range of cells) that were created using the Create Name feature in the Define Name dialog box. Select **Insert**, point at **Name**, and then select **Define**. All the range names that you created appear in the Names in Workbook list.

→ Inserting a Range Name into a Formula or Function

As previously discussed in this lesson, range names make it easy for you to specify a range of cells in a formula or function. To insert a range name into a formula or function, follow these steps:

1 Click in the cell where you want to place the formula or function.

2 Type the formula or function (begin the formula or function with the equal sign).

3 When you are ready to insert the range name into the formula or function, select the **Insert** menu, point at **Name**, and then select **Paste**. The Paste Name dialog box appears (see Figure 11.4).

Figure 11.4 Use the Paste Name dialog box to insert a range name into a formula or function.

4 Select the range name you want to place in the formula or function, and then click **OK**.

5 Finish typing the formula or function (including the appropriate operators).

6 Press **Enter** to place the formula or function into the cell and return the calculated value.

Timesaver tip

Type the Name of a Range When you are creating a formula or function using a range name and you remember what that range name is, you can type it into the formula or function. You don't have to use the Paste Name dialog box.

12 Inserting and Removing Cells, Rows, and Columns

In this lesson, you learn how to rearrange the data in your worksheet by adding and removing cells, rows, and columns. You also learn how to adjust the width of your columns and the height of your rows to make the best use of the worksheet space.

→ Inserting Rows and Columns

As you edit and enhance your worksheets, you might need to add rows or columns within the worksheet. Inserting entire rows and columns into your worksheet is very straightforward. Follow these steps:

1 To insert a single row or column, select a cell to the right of where you want to insert a column or below where you want to insert a row.

To insert multiple columns or rows, select the number of columns or rows you want to insert. To insert columns, drag over the column letters at the top of the worksheet. To insert rows, drag over the row numbers. For example, select three column letters or row numbers to insert three rows or columns.

2 Select the **Insert** menu, and then select **Rows** or **Columns**. Excel inserts rows above your selection and columns to the left of your selection. The inserted rows or columns contain the same formatting as the cells (or rows and columns) you selected in step 1. Figure 12.1 shows a worksheet to which additional columns have been added.

As you can see, when you insert rows or columns, the Insert Options shortcut icon appears to the right of the inserted columns or below inserted rows. Use the Insert Options menu to specify the column or row from which the new column or row should copy its formatting.

For example, in the case of inserted columns, you can choose to
copy the formatting from the column to the right or left of the inserted
column or columns, or you can choose to clear the formatting in the
inserted columns.

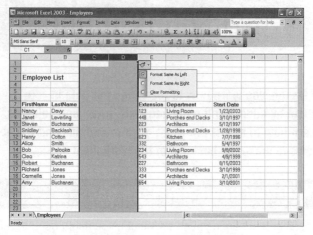

Figure 12.1 Columns can easily be inserted into an Excel worksheet.

Timesaver tip

Fast Insert To quickly insert rows or columns, select one or more rows or
columns, right-click one of them, and choose **Insert** from the shortcut menu.

→ Removing Rows and Columns

When you delete a row in your worksheet, the rows below the deleted
row move up to fill the space. When you delete a column, the columns
to the right shift left.

Follow these steps to delete a row or column:

1 Click the row number or column letter of the row or column you
want to delete. You can select more than one row or column by
dragging over the row numbers or column letters.

2 Select the **Edit** menu and then select **Delete**. Excel deletes the rows or columns and renumbers the remaining rows and columns sequentially. All cell references in formulas and functions are updated appropriately.

→ Inserting Cells

Although inserting rows and columns makes it easy to dramatically change the layout of a worksheet, on occasion you might need to insert only a cell or cells into a worksheet. Inserting cells causes the data in existing cells to shift down a row or over a column to create a space for the new cells.

Important

Watch Your Formulas and Functions Inserting cells into a worksheet can throw off the cell references in formulas and functions. Double-check your formulas and functions after inserting cells to make sure that the calculations are acting upon the appropriate cell addresses.

12

insert a single cell or a group of cells, follow these steps:

1 Select the area where you want the new cells inserted. Excel inserts the same number of cells as you select.

2 Select the **Insert** menu and then select **Cells**. The Insert dialog box appears (see Figure 12.2).

Figure 12.2 You can insert cells into a worksheet using the Insert dialog box.

3 Select **Shift Cells Right** or **Shift Cells Down** (or you can choose to have an entire row or column inserted).

4 Click **OK**. Excel inserts the cells and shifts the adjacent cells in the direction you specify.

You will find that inserting cells is useful if you have entered rows of information and have mismatched data, such as a customer's name with someone else's order information. Inserting a couple of cells enables you to quickly edit the data without having to delete data or insert a new row.

Timesaver tip

Drag Insert Cells A quick way to insert cells is to select the number of cells you want, hold down the **Shift** key, and then drag the fill handle up, down, left, or right to set the position of the new cells.

→ Removing Cells

You already learned about deleting the data in cells back in Lesson 8, "Editing Worksheets," and you learned that you could also delete cells from a worksheet. Eliminating cells from the worksheet rather than just clearing their contents means that the cells surrounding the deleted cells in the worksheet are moved to fill the gap that is created. Remove cells only if you want the other cells in the worksheet to shift to new positions. Otherwise, just delete the data in the cells or type new data into the cells.

If you want to remove cells from a worksheet, use the following steps:

1 Select the cell or range of cells you want to remove.

2 Open the **Edit** menu and choose **Delete**. The Delete dialog box appears (see Figure 12.3).

Figure 12.3 Use the Delete dialog box to specify how the gap left by the deleted cells should be filled.

3 Select **Shift Cells Left** or **Shift Cells Up** to specify how the remaining cells in the worksheet should move to fill the gap left by the deleted cells.

4 Click **OK**. Surrounding cells are shifted to fill the gap left by the deleted cells.

As with inserting cells, you should check the cell references in your formulas and functions after removing cells from the worksheet. Be sure that your calculations are referencing the appropriate cells on the worksheet.

→ Adjusting Column Width and Row Height with a Mouse

It doesn't take very long when you are working in Excel to realize that the default column width of 8.43 characters doesn't accommodate long text entries or values that have been formatted as currency or other numeric formats. You can adjust the width of a column quickly using the mouse.

You can also adjust row heights, if you want, using the mouse. However, your row heights will adjust to any font size changes that you make to data held in a particular row. Row heights also adjust if you wrap text entries within them (see Lesson 9, "Changing How Numbers and Text Look," for more about wrapping text). You will probably find that you need to adjust column widths in your worksheets far more often than row heights.

> ## Important
>
> **What Is ########?** When you format a value in a cell with numeric formatting and Excel cannot display the result in the cell because of the column width, Excel displays ######## in the cell. This lets you know that you need to adjust the column width so that it can accommodate the entry and its formatting.

To adjust a column width with the mouse, place the mouse pointer on the right border of the column. A sizing tool appears, as shown in Figure 12.4. Drag the column border to the desired width. You can also adjust the column width to automatically accommodate the widest entry within a column; just double-click the sizing tool. This is called AutoFit, and the column adjusts according to the widest entry.

Sizing tool

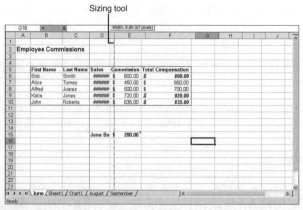

Figure 12.4 Use the column width sizing tool to adjust the width of a column.

If you want to adjust several columns at once, select the columns. Place the mouse on any of the column borders and drag to increase or decrease the width. Each selected column is adjusted to the width you select.

Changing row heights is similar to adjusting column widths. Place the mouse on the lower border of a row and drag the sizing tool to increase or decrease the row height. To change the height of multiple rows, select the rows and then drag the border of any of the selected rows to the desired height.

→ Using the Format Menu for Precise Control

If you want to precisely specify the width of a column or columns or the height of a row or rows, you can enter specific sizes using a dialog box. This provides you with a little more control than just dragging a row height or column width.

To specify a column width, follow these steps:

1 Select the columns you want to change.

2 Select the **Format** menu, point at **Column**, and then select **Width**. The Column Width dialog box appears (see Figure 12.5).

Figure 12.5 Column widths can also be specified in the Column Width dialog box.

3 Type the column width into the dialog box (the width is measured in number of characters).

4 Click **OK**. Your column(s) width is adjusted accordingly.

Adjusting row heights is similar to adjusting column widths. Select the row or rows, and then select the **Format** menu, point at **Rows**, and select **Height.** In the Row Height dialog box that appears, type in the row height and then click **OK**.

12

13 Managing Your Worksheets

In this lesson, you learn how to add and delete worksheets within workbooks. You also learn how to copy, move, and rename worksheets.

→ Selecting Worksheets

By default, each workbook consists of three worksheets whose names appear on tabs at the bottom of the Excel window. You can add or delete worksheets as desired. One advantage of having multiple worksheets within a workbook is that it enables you to organize your data into logical chunks. Another advantage of having separate worksheets for your data is that you can easily reorganize the worksheets (and the associated data) in a workbook.

Before you learn about the details of inserting, deleting, and copying worksheets, you should know how to select one or more worksheets. Selecting a single worksheet is a method of moving from worksheet to worksheet in a workbook.

Selecting multiple worksheets in a workbook, however, is another story. Selecting multiple workbooks enables you to apply the same AutoFormatting or cell formatting to more than one worksheet at a time. This is particularly useful in cases where you might have several worksheets in a workbook that will end up looking very much the same. For example, you might have a workbook that contains four worksheets—each of the worksheets serving as a quarterly summary. Because the design of these worksheets is similar, applying formatting to more than one sheet at a time enables you to keep the sheets consistent in appearance.

To select a worksheet or worksheets, perform one of the following actions:

- To select a single worksheet, click its tab. The tab becomes highlighted to show that the worksheet is selected.

- To select several neighboring or adjacent worksheets, click the tab of the first worksheet in the group and then hold down the **Shift** key and click the tab of the last worksheet in the group. Each worksheet tab will be highlighted (but only the first sheet selected will be visible).

- To select several nonadjacent worksheets, hold down the **Ctrl** key and click each worksheet's tab.

If you select two or more worksheets, they remain selected as a group until you ungroup them. To ungroup worksheets, do one of the following:

- Right-click one of the selected worksheets and choose **Ungroup Sheets**.

- Hold down the **Shift** key and click the tab of the active worksheet.

- Click any worksheet tab to deselect all the other worksheets.

→ Inserting Worksheets

When you create a new workbook, it contains three worksheets. You can easily add additional worksheets to a workbook.

Timesaver tip

Start with More Sheets You can change the default number of worksheets Excel places in a new workbook by opening the **Tools** menu, selecting **Options**, clicking the **General** tab, and then changing the number in the **Sheets in New Workbook** option. Click **OK** to save your changes. The maximum value for the number of worksheets in a workbook is determined by the amount of memory on your computer. If you use more than 20 worksheets in a workbook and the worksheets are full of data, you might find that Excel's overall performance starts to slow down.

Follow these steps to add a worksheet to a workbook:

1 Select the worksheet that you want to be to the right of the inserted worksheet. For example, if you select the August sheet shown in Figure 13.1, the new sheet will be inserted to the left of August.

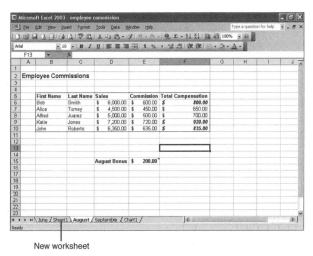

New worksheet

Figure 13.1 Excel inserts the new worksheet to the left of the active worksheet.

2 Select the **Insert** menu.

3 Select **Worksheet**. Excel inserts the new worksheet to the right of the previously selected worksheet.

Timesaver tip

Use the Shortcut Menu A faster way to work with worksheets is to right-click the worksheet's tab. This brings up a shortcut menu that enables you to insert, delete, rename, move, copy, or select all worksheets.

→ Deleting Worksheets

If you find that you have a worksheet you no longer need, or if you plan to use only one worksheet of the three that Excel puts into each workbook by default, you can remove the unwanted worksheets. Here's how you remove a worksheet:

1 Select the worksheet(s) you want to delete.

2 Select the **Edit** menu and then select **Delete Sheet**.

3 If the sheet contains data, a dialog box appears, asking you to confirm the deletion. Click **Delete** to delete the sheet. You will lose any data that the sheet contained.

You can delete multiple sheets if you want. Use the techniques discussed earlier in this lesson to select multiple sheets, and then use steps 2 and 3 in this section to delete the sheets.

→ Moving and Copying Worksheets

You can move or copy worksheets within a workbook or from one workbook to another. Copying a worksheet enables you to copy the formatting of the sheet and other items, such as the column labels and the row labels. Follow these steps:

1 Select the worksheet or worksheets you want to move or copy. If you want to move or copy worksheets from one workbook to another, be sure the target workbook is open.

2 Select the **Edit** menu and choose **Move or Copy Sheet**. The Move or Copy dialog box appears, as shown in Figure 13.2.

Figure 13.2 The Move or Copy dialog box asks where you want to copy or move a worksheet.

3 To move the worksheets to a different workbook, be sure that workbook is open, and then select that workbook's name from the To Book drop-down list. If you want to move or copy the worksheets to a new workbook, select (**New Book**) in the To Book drop-down list. Excel creates a new workbook and then copies or moves the worksheets to it.

4 In the Before Sheet list box, choose the worksheet you want to follow the selected worksheets.

5 To move the selected worksheet, skip to step 6. To copy the selected worksheets instead of moving them, select the **Create a Copy** option.

6 Select **OK**. The selected worksheets are copied or moved as specified.

Moving a Worksheet Within a Workbook with Drag and Drop

A fast way to copy or move worksheets within a workbook is to use drag and drop. First, select the tab of the worksheet(s) you want to copy or move.

Move the mouse pointer over one of the selected tabs, click and hold the mouse button, and drag the tab where you want it moved. To copy the worksheet, hold down the **Ctrl** key while dragging. When you release the mouse button, the worksheet is copied or moved.

13

Moving or Copying a Worksheet Between Workbooks with Drag and Drop

You can also use the drag-and-drop feature to quickly copy or move worksheets between workbooks.

1 Open the workbooks you want to use for the copy or move.

2 Select **Window** and select **Arrange**. The Arrange dialog box opens.

3 You can arrange the different workbook windows horizontally, vertically, tiled, or cascaded in the Excel application window. For more than two open workbooks, your best selection is probably the **Tiled** option.

4 After making your selection, click **OK** to arrange the workbook windows within the Excel application window. Figure 13.3 shows three open workbooks that have been tiled.

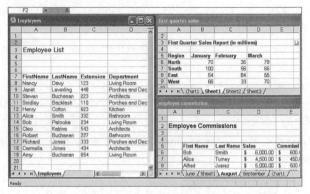

Figure 13.3 You can arrange multiple workbooks in the Excel window and then move or copy worksheets.

5 Select the tab of the worksheet(s) you want to copy or move.

6 Move the mouse pointer over one of the selected tabs, click and hold the mouse button, and drag the tab where you want it moved. To copy the worksheet, hold down the **Ctrl** key while dragging.

7 When you release the mouse button, the worksheet is copied or moved.

Timesaver tip

Compare Workbooks Side-by-Side You can display two workbooks side-by-side for a quick comparison of the data. With the workbooks open in Excel, select **Window** and then **Compare Side by Side**. If only one other workbook is open, the workbook name will appear as part of the Compare Side by Side command on the menu. When you're working with multiple open workbooks, a Compare Side by Side dialog box will open listing the other open workbooks. Select the workbook for comparison and then click **OK**.

→ Changing Worksheet Tab Names

By default, all worksheets are named SheetX, where X is a number starting with the number 1. So that you'll have a better idea of the information each sheet contains, you should change the names that appear on the tabs. Here's how to do it:

1 Double-click the tab of the worksheet you want to rename. The current name is highlighted.

2 Type a new name for the worksheet and press **Enter**. Excel replaces the default name with the name you type.

13

14 Printing Your Workbook

In this lesson, you learn how to preview your print jobs, repeat row and column headings on pages, and add headers and footers to your worksheets. You also learn how to print an entire workbook and large worksheets.

→ Previewing a Print Job

After you've finished a particular worksheet and want to send it to the printer, you might want to take a quick look at how the worksheet will look on the printed page. You will find that worksheets don't always print the way that they look on the screen.

To preview a print job, select the **File** menu and then select **Print Preview,** or click the **Print Preview** button on the Standard toolbar. Your workbook appears in the same format that it will be in when sent to the printer (see Figure 14.1).

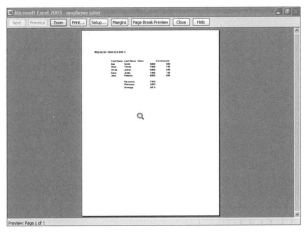

Figure 14..1 By previewing the worksheet, you can determine which page layout attributes need adjusting.

From this view you can zoom in on any area of the preview by clicking it with the mouse pointer (which looks like a magnifying glass). Or use the **Zoom** button on the Print Preview toolbar.

Timesaver tip

Access Print Preview from Other Dialog Boxes The Page Setup and Print dialog boxes explained later in this lesson also include a Preview button, so you can check any last-minute changes you made in either dialog box without having to close the box first.

When you have finished previewing your worksheet, you can print the worksheet by clicking the **Print** button, or you can return to the worksheet by clicking **Close**.

→ Changing the Page Setup

After you preview your worksheet, you might want to adjust page attributes or change the way the page is set up for printing. For example, you might want to print the column and row labels on every page of the printout. This is particularly useful for large worksheets that span several pages; then you don't have to keep looking back to the first page of the printout to determine what the column headings are.

Printing column and row labels and other worksheet page attributes, such as scaling a worksheet to print out on a single page or adding headers or footers to a worksheet printout, are handled in the Page Setup dialog box. To access this dialog box, select the **File** menu and then select **Page Setup** (see Figure 14.2).

The following sections provide information on some of the most common page setup attributes that you will work with before printing your Excel worksheets.

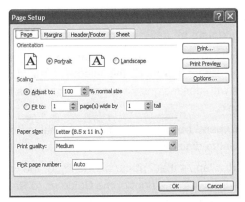

Figure 14.2 Access the Page Setup dialog box to make sure your worksheet page is set to print correctly.

Printing Column and Row Labels on Every Page

Excel provides a way for you to select labels and titles that are located on the top edge and left side of a large worksheet and to print them on every page of the printout. This option is useful when a worksheet is too wide to print on a single page. If you don't use this option, the extra columns or rows are printed on subsequent pages without any descriptive labels.

Follow these steps to print column or row labels on every page:

1 Select the **File** menu and then select **Page Setup**. The Page Setup dialog box appears.

2 Click the **Sheet** tab to display the Sheet options (see Figure 14.3).

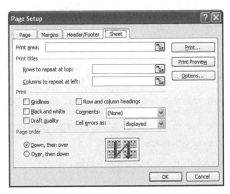

Figure 14.3 Use the Sheet tab to specify headings you want to repeat in the printout.

3 To repeat column labels and a worksheet title, click the **Shrink** button to the right of the Rows to Repeat at Top text box.

4 Drag over the rows that you want to print on every page. A dashed line border surrounds the selected area, and absolute cell references with dollar signs ($) appear in the Rows to Repeat at Top text box.

5 Click the **Expand** button on the collapsed dialog box to expand the Page Setup dialog box.

6 To repeat row labels that appear on the left of the worksheet, click the **Shrink** button to the right of the Columns to Repeat at Left text box. Excel reduces the Page Setup dialog box.

7 Select the columns that contain the row labels you want to repeat.

8 Click the **Expand** button to return again to the Page Setup dialog box.

9 To print your worksheet, click **Print** to display the Print dialog box. Then click **OK**.

Timesaver tip

Select Your Print Area Carefully If you select rows or columns to repeat, and those rows or columns are part of your print area, the selected rows or columns might print twice. To fix this, select your print area again, leaving out the rows or columns you're repeating.

Scaling a Worksheet to Fit on a Page

If your worksheet is too large to print on one page even after you change the orientation and margins, consider using the **Fit To** option. This option shrinks the worksheet to make it fit on the specified number of pages. You can specify the document's width and height.

Follow these steps to scale a worksheet to fit on a page:

1 Select the **File** menu and then select **Page Setup**. The Page Setup dialog box appears.

2 Click the **Page** tab to display the Page options.

3 In the Fit to XX Page(s) Wide by XX Tall text boxes, enter the number of pages into which you want Excel to fit your data (don't try to cram too much information on a page; this will make the font very small and the data difficult to read).

4 Click **OK** to close the Page Setup dialog box and return to your worksheet, or click the **Print** button in the Page Setup dialog box to display the Print dialog box, and then click **OK** to print your worksheet.

Timesaver tip

Change the Page Orientation The Page tab of the Page Setup dialog box also enables you to change the orientation of the worksheet from Portrait to Landscape. Landscape orientation is useful if you have a worksheet with a large number of columns.

Adding Headers and Footers

Excel enables you to add headers and footers to your worksheets that will appear at the top and bottom of every page of the printout (respectively). The information can include any text, as well as page numbers, the current date and time, the workbook filename, and the worksheet tab name.

14

You can choose the headers and footers that Excel suggests, or you can include any text plus special commands to control the appearance of the header or footer. For example, you can apply bold, italic, or underline to the header or footer text. You can also left-align, center, or right-align your text in a header or footer (see Lesson 9, "Changing How Numbers and Text Look," for more information).

To add headers and footers, follow these steps:

1 Select the **File** menu and then select **Page Setup**. The Page Setup dialog box appears. Click the **Header/Footer** tab on the dialog box (see Figure 14.4).

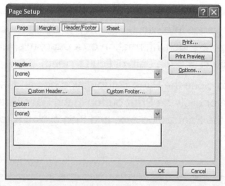

Figure 14.4 Add headers and footers with Header/Footer options.

2 To select a header, click the **Header** drop-down arrow. Excel displays a list of suggested header information. Scroll through the list and click a header you want. The sample header appears at the top of the Header/Footer tab.

Timesaver tip

Don't See One You Like? If none of the suggested headers or footers suit you, click the **Custom Header** or **Custom Footer** button and enter your own information.

3 To select a footer, click the **Footer** drop-down arrow. Excel displays a list of suggested footer information. Scroll through the list and click a footer you want. The sample footer appears at the bottom of the Header/Footer tab.

4 Click **OK** to close the Page Setup dialog box and return to your worksheet, or click the **Print** button to display the Print dialog box and click **OK** to print your worksheet.

Timesaver tip

Don't Want Headers or Footers Any More? To remove the header and/or footer, choose (**None**) in the **Header** and/or **Footer** lists.

Setting Sheet Settings

The Sheet tab of the Page Setup dialog box allows you to specify a number of print settings such as the area of the worksheet to be printed and whether or not gridlines should be included on the printout. Figure 14.5 shows the Sheet tab.

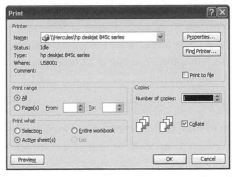

Figure 14.5 The Sheet tab gives you control over a number of print-related parameters.

Settings related to printing that are controlled on the Sheet tab are as follows:

■ **Print area**—You can specify what part of a worksheet is printed. Click the Shrink button to the right of the Print area box and then select the area to print. Press Enter to return to the dialog box.

■ **Print titles**—You can specify columns or rows to be printed on each page of the printout. This is used to repeat column headings or row headings on each page of a large worksheet. Use the appropriate shrink button to specify the range of the rows or columns to repeat.

■ **Print settings**—The Print area of the Sheets tab allows you to specify what should be placed on the printed pages. This includes check boxes for gridlines, black and white, or draft printout and row and column headings (the number and letter designations of the row and columns).

■ **Page order**—This allows you to specify how subsequent pages are created as a worksheet that will not fit on a single page is printed. The default **Down, and then over** moves down the worksheet, printing additional pages; when it reaches the bottom of the sheet it moves over to continue printing the data. The **Over, and then**

14

down option moves across the worksheet from left to right printing pages and then moves down as it continues printing the worksheet.

After you have set the options of the Sheet tab, you can close the Page Setup dialog box. Click **OK** to close it.

→ Printing Your Workbook

After adjusting the page settings for the worksheet and previewing your data, it is time to print. You can print selected data, selected sheets, or the entire workbook.

To print your workbook, follow these steps:

1 If you want to print a portion of the worksheet, select the range of cells you want to print. To print only a chart, click it (you learn about creating charts in Lesson 15, "Creating Charts"). If you want to print one or more worksheets within the workbook, select the worksheet tabs (see Lesson 13, "Managing Your Worksheets"). To print the entire workbook, skip this step.

2 Select the **File** menu and then select **Print** (or press **Ctrl+P**). The Print dialog box appears, as shown in Figure 14.6.

Timesaver tip

Print Using the Default Settings If you click the **Print** button (instead of using the **File** menu and clicking **Print**), Excel prints your current worksheet without letting you make any selections.

3 Select the options you would like to use:

- **Print Range**—Enables you to print one or more pages. For example, if the selected print area contains 15 pages and you want to print only pages 5–10, select **Page(s)** and then type the numbers of the first and last page you want to print into the **From** and **To** boxes.

- **Print What**—Enables you to print the currently selected cells, the selected worksheets, or the entire workbook.

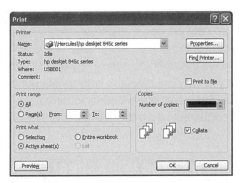

Figure 14.6 In the Print dialog box, select your printer and a page range to print.

- **Copies**—Enables you to print more than one copy of the selection, worksheet, or workbook.

- **Collate**—Enables you to print a complete copy of the selection, worksheet, or workbook before the first page of the next copy is printed. This option is available when you print multiple copies.

4 Click **OK** to print your selection, worksheet, or workbook.

While your job is printing, you can continue working in Excel. If the printer is working on another job that you (or someone else, in the case of a network printer) sent, Windows holds your current job until the printer is ready for it.

Sometimes you might want to delete a job while it is printing or before it prints. For example, suppose you think of other numbers to add to the worksheet or realize that you forgot to format some text; you'll want to fix these things before you print the file. To display the print queue and delete a print job, follow these steps:

1 Double-click the **Printer** icon in the Windows system tray (at the far right of the taskbar), and the print queue appears.

2 Click the job you want to delete.

3 Select the **Document** menu and then select **Cancel Printing**, or just press **Delete**.

> To delete all the files from the print queue, open the **Printer** menu and select **Purge Print Documents**. This cancels the print jobs but doesn't delete the files from your computer.

The amount of control you have over printing documents depends on whether or not you are printing to a printer directly connected to your computer or a networked printer. In the case of a directly connected computer, you have the ability to cancel any and all print jobs. On a network printer you may not have the appropriate rights to purge or delete print jobs. See your network administrator if you cannot delete your own print documents from the print queue.

→ Selecting a Large Worksheet Print Area

You don't always have to print an entire worksheet; instead, you can easily tell Excel what part of the worksheet you want to print by selecting the print area yourself. If the area you select is too large to fit on one page, no problem; Excel breaks it into multiple pages. When you do not select a print area yourself, Excel prints either the entire worksheet or the entire workbook, depending on the options set in the Print dialog box.

To select a print area, follow these steps:

1 Click the upper-left cell of the range you want to print.

2 Drag downward and to the right until the range you want is selected.

3 Select the **File** menu, point at **Print Area**, and then select **Set Print Area**.

To remove the print area so you can print the entire worksheet again, select the **File** menu, select **Print Area**, and select **Clear Print Area**.

→ Adjusting Page Breaks

When you print a workbook, Excel determines the page breaks based on the paper size, the margins, and the selected print area. To make the pages look better and to break information in logical places, you might want to override the automatic page breaks with your own breaks. However, before you add page breaks, try these options:

- Adjust the widths of individual columns to make the best use of space.
- Consider printing the workbook using the Landscape orientation.
- Change the left, right, top, and bottom margins to smaller values.

After trying these options, if you still want to insert page breaks, Excel offers you an option of previewing exactly where the page breaks appear and then adjusting them. Follow these steps:

1 Select the **View** menu and select **Page Break Preview**.

2 If a message appears telling you how to adjust page breaks, click **OK**. Your worksheet is displayed with page breaks, as shown in Figure 14.7.

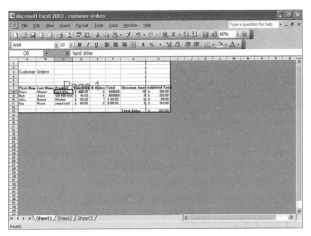

Figure 14.7 Check your page breaks before printing your worksheet.

3 To move a page break, drag the blue line to the desired location. To delete a page break, drag it off the screen.

To insert a page break, move to the first cell in the column to the right of where you want the page break inserted, or move to the row below where you want the break inserted. For example, to insert a page break between columns G and H, move to cell H1. To insert a page break between rows 24 and 25, move to cell A25. Then, open the **Insert** menu and select **Page Break**. A dashed line appears to the left of the selected column or above the selected row.

4 To exit Page Break Preview and return to your normal worksheet view, open the **View** menu and select **Normal**.

Once you have modified the page breaks, you may want to take a look at the pages in Print Preview (click the **Print Preview** button on the Standard toolbar). This allows you to see how well balanced the pages are in terms of the amount of printed data and white space on the page.

15 | Creating Charts

In this lesson, you learn how to create graphical representations (charts) of workbook data.

→ Understanding Charting Terminology

Charts enable you to create a graphical representation of data in a worksheet. You can use charts to make data more understandable to people who view your printed worksheets. Before you start creating charts, you should familiarize yourself with the following terminology:

- **Data Series**—The bars, pie wedges, lines, or other elements that represent plotted values in a chart. For example, a chart might show a set of similar bars that reflects a series of values for the same item. The bars in the same data series would all have the same pattern. If you have more than one pattern of bars, each pattern would represent a separate data series. For example, charting the sales for Territory 1 versus Territory 2 would require two data series—one for each territory. Often, data series correspond to rows of data in your worksheet (although they can correspond to columns of data if that is how you have arranged the information in your worksheet).

- **Categories**—Categories reflect the number of elements in a series. You might have two data series that compare the sales of two territories and four categories that compare these sales over four quarters. Some charts have only one category, and others have several. Categories normally correspond to the columns in your worksheet, with the category labels coming from the column headings.

- **Axis**—One side of a chart. A two-dimensional chart has an x-axis (horizontal) and a y-axis (vertical). The x-axis contains the data series and categories in the chart. If you have more than one category, the x-axis often contains labels that define what each category represents. The y-axis reflects the values of the bars, lines, or plot points. In a three-dimensional chart, the z-axis represents the vertical plane, and the x-axis (distance) and y-axis (width) represent the two sides on the floor of the chart.

- **Legend**—Defines the separate series of a chart. For example, the legend for a pie chart shows what each piece of the pie represents.

- **Gridlines**—Typically, gridlines appear along the y-axis of the chart. The y-axis is where your values are displayed, although they can emanate from the x-axis as well (the x-axis is where label information normally appears on the chart). Gridlines help you determine a point's exact value.

→ Working with Different Chart Types

With Excel, you can create many types of charts. Some common chart types are shown in Figure 15.1. The chart type you choose depends on the kind of data you're trying to chart and on how you want to present that data. The following are the major chart types and their purposes:

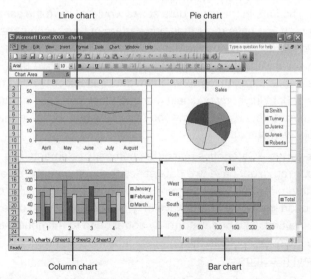

Figure 15.1 Excel chart types enable you to analyze and present your data.

- **Pie**—Use this chart type to show the relationship among parts of a whole.

- **Bar**—Use this chart type to compare values at a given point in time.

- **Column**—Similar to the bar chart; use this chart type to emphasize the difference between items.

- **Line**—Use this chart type to emphasize trends and the change of values over time.

- **Scatter**—Similar to a line chart; use this chart type to emphasize the difference between two sets of values.

- **Area**—Similar to the line chart; use this chart type to emphasize the amount of change in values over time.

Most of these basic chart types also come in three-dimensional varieties. In addition to looking more professional than the standard flat charts, 3D charts can often help your audience distinguish between different sets of data.

→ Creating and Saving a Chart

You can place your new chart on the same worksheet that contains the chart data (an embedded chart) or on a separate worksheet (a chart sheet). If you create an embedded chart, it is typically printed side by side with your worksheet data. Embedded charts are useful for showing the actual data and its graphical representation side by side. If you create a chart on a separate worksheet, however, you can print it independently. Both types of charts are linked to the worksheet data that they represent, so when you change the data, the chart is automatically updated.

15

The **Chart Wizard** button on the Standard toolbar enables you to quickly create a chart. To use the Chart Wizard, follow these steps:

1 Select the data you want to chart. If you typed column or row labels (such as Qtr 1, Qtr 2, and so on) that you want included in the chart, be sure you select those, too.

2 Click the **Chart Wizard** button on the Standard toolbar.

3 The **Chart Wizard – Step 1 of 4** dialog box appears (see Figure 15.2). Select a **Chart Type** and a **Chart Sub-Type** (a variation on the selected chart type). Click **Next**.

4 Next, Excel asks whether the selected range is correct. You can correct the range by typing a new range or by clicking the **Shrink** button (located at the right end of the **Data Range** text box) and selecting the range you want to use.

5 By default, Excel assumes that your different data series are stored in rows. You can change this to columns if necessary by clicking the **Series in Columns** option. When you're ready for the next step, click **Next**.

Figure 15.2 Choose the chart type using the Chart Wizard.

6 Click the various tabs to change options for your chart (see Figure 15.3). For example, you can delete the legend by clicking the **Legend** tab and deselecting **Show Legend**. You can add a chart title on the **Titles** tab. Add data labels (labels that display the actual value being represented by each bar, line, and so on) by clicking the **Data Labels** tab. When you finish making changes, click **Next**.

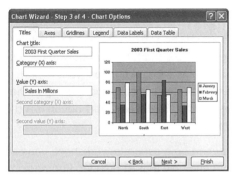

Figure 15.3 Select from various chart appearance options.

7 Finally, Excel asks whether you want to embed the chart (as an object) in the current worksheet (or any other existing worksheet in the workbook) or if you want to create a new worksheet for it. Make your selection and click the **Finish** button. Your completed chart appears.

Timesaver tip

Create a Chart Fast! To create a chart quickly, select the data you want to use and press **F11**. Excel creates a column chart (the default chart type) on its own sheet. You can then customize the chart as needed.

15

The charts you create are part of the current workbook. To save a chart, simply save the workbook that contains the chart.

→ Moving and Resizing a Chart

To move an embedded chart, click anywhere in the chart area and drag it to the new location. To change the size of a chart, select the chart and then drag one of its handles (the black squares that border the chart). Drag a corner handle to change the height and width, or drag a side handle to change only one dimension. (Note that you can't really resize a chart that is on a sheet by itself.)

→ Printing a Chart

If a chart is an embedded chart, it will print when you print the worksheet that contains the chart. If you want to print just the embedded chart, click it to select it, and then open the **File** menu and select **Print**. Be sure the **Selected Chart** option is turned on. Then, click **OK** to print the chart.

If you created a chart on a separate worksheet, you can print the chart separately by printing only that worksheet. For more information about printing, refer to Lesson 14, "Printing Your Workbook."